Moving Between Times

Modernity and Postmodernity:
A Christian View

Brian Carrell

The
DeepSight
Trust

A New Zealand Initiative for Religion and Cultures

© 1998 by Brian Ruane Carrell
All rights reserved

ISBN 0-9582012-1-8
First published 1998
The DeepSight Trust
PO Box 87-362, Meadowbank
Auckland, New Zealand.

Typeset in Berkeley and Frutiger.
Design and artwork by Streamline Creative Ltd, Auckland.
Cover design by Heather Ball.

Printed by Colorcraft Ltd, Hong Kong.

I dedicate this book to the faithful clergy and lay leaders, women and men, with whom I have worked over many years in the Anglican Diocese of Wellington, New Zealand, and particularly to the leadership given by Archbishop Brian Davis over these years.

As this book went to print, the death in England was announced of Bishop Lesslie Newbigin, doyen of the worldwide Gospel & Culture movement. In the years following his retirement from ministry in India, he made an unparalleled contribution to the concerns that have come to be expressed as 'Gospel & Culture'. Both the author and DeepSight Trust wish to acknowledge their debt to the inspiration and insights they received from Lesslie Newbigin. They dedicate this book to his memory and themselves to the tasks in which he gave such a splendid lead.

"The truth is that we are in a time of transition, an in-between period when the old is dying and the new has yet to be born. The values, assumptions and structures that have governed us for so long have come to their logical end, and now we find ourselves at a dead end. But new values, patterns and institutions have not yet emerged. We are caught in the middle, stranded between paradigms."

Jim Wallis
The Soul of Politics

Contents

Foreword

The cultural assumptions and values of humanistic modernism have increasingly dominated Western societies and indeed the whole world. Modernity has not only challenged and undermined the authority of the Church as a purveyor of truth. It has also been a corrupting force from within, when the Church, in order to appear more 'relevant', has too readily sought to accommodate to its outlook.

The end of this tumultuous century witnessed modernist assumptions under attack by 'postmodernist' thinkers and commentators. It is necessary to be aware of this critical intellectual and cultural shift to understand the world. Those in the Church as well as those in society need to know what is happening to grasp the new opportunities and insightful observations not so conveniently accessible.

Bishop Carrell is well equipped for this task. He has a deep understanding of his subject, the fruit of many years of extensive reading, reflection and study. He has had an international experience of the Church and its mission and, as a bishop, has a first-hand working knowledge of a major Church in New Zealand.

Moving Between Times will be a valuable resource for those seeking to understand more fully the attitudes, ideas and values that shape Western society today, and will continue to impact on all peoples of the world in the third millennium. It provides valuable insights for the mission strategists of the Church, for all who are responding to Christ's call to be salt and light in the world, and indeed for every concerned citizen.

I am delighted to have the opportunity to warmly commend this book and to thank its author for his gift to us all.

Brian Davis

Napier, April 1998

The Most Reverend B.N. Davis, MA., C.N.Z.M., was until mid-1997 Archbishop and Primate of the Anglican Church in Aotearoa, New Zealand and Polynesia.

Preface

During the second half of 1996 a study leave entitlement enabled me to travel to the United Kingdom to spend most of a term in Cambridge. My purpose was to research, at a deeper level than snatched reading and reflection on the other side of the world permitted, the issues relating to modernity, postmodernity and the Gospel, particularly as they affected my own ministry as an Anglican Bishop. For several years I had been steadily working away at these questions, largely on my own, but with the stimulation of a Gospel & Culture group, drawn from several different Christian denominations in the area, that had been meeting monthly since 1991 in our home in Palmerston North.

I arrived with no firm intention of writing a book. But I quickly came to see how important this subject was becoming for the whole Church in the Western world, how urgent was the need to understand the issues in order to discern the way ahead, and yet also what a vast gulf existed between the learned (and sometimes inaccessible) tomes of academia on the subject and the often superficial or piecemeal treatment of it more readily available in popular magazine articles. There was little in between.

My intention has been that of a theological entrepreneur, providing a bridge between these learned publications and those bewildered church people who want to know what is happening to their world and how this relates to their faith, yet who either cannot obtain or are unable to comprehend much of the writing now available on the subject.

This book, therefore, offers a 'beginner's guide' to modernity and postmodernity in order to help in understanding how these current social and cultural shifts in the Western world are affecting Christian mission and ministry. I write out of a deep conviction that our Western societies have been changing so fundamentally that today the world in which our Churches stand bears little resemblance to the world our grandparents knew – or to the world for which most of our Churches and their structures and styles were originally designed.

There has been a growing stiffening in resistance to the Gospel of Jesus Christ – or at the very least a sense of the irrelevance of much of the apparatus and style of the traditional Churches to the world as it is experienced in the West today. This has become evident in a steady drift away from, and even open rejection of, older Christian values and public morality. The boundaries of the playing field and the rules of the game both appear to have been changed while the rest of us were busy chasing the ball across the field.

My intention has been to make this guide deep and detailed enough to do justice to the great movements of thought and change in Western culture and society now referred to as modernity and postmodernity. At the same time I have tried to keep the style crisp and absorbing enough to hold the interest and attention of the reader, especially by constant reference to contemporary and familiar situations. Of necessity, these largely relate to the scene in the Southern Hemisphere, and more especially the expression of Western culture encountered in New Zealand. However, I expect readers in other countries will readily recognize equivalent examples in their own areas.

My original focus in setting out to write this book was on the Church, but subsequently the work has been adopted by the DeepSight project in New Zealand as a basic reference text for generally understanding modern and postmodern developments within Western culture. This has much enlarged the book's prospective constituency beyond the Christian Church. Since we are all caught up together in this confused, contemporary, post-Christendom situation, I hope this work may serve all who ask questions and seek answers concerning the world they live in today, whether or not they identify themselves as Christians, and wherever on the globe they happen to live in a Western society.

Brian Carrell

April 1998

CHAPTER ONE

Signs of a Massive
Western Culture Shift

Many people in the West feel that they have been let down. The accumulated gains of a century of triumphant technology and great social reforms should have been yielding unparalleled joy and tranquillity. Yet as the century draws to a close both Church and society are experiencing much unanticipated pain. The bright hopes of yesteryear have not been fulfilled. Something has gone wrong.

The Pain of the World

Social pains of various kinds, both old and new, continue to be experienced throughout the Western world. Though these may differ in detail from nation to nation, more surprizing is how pain is being experienced in similar ways in different countries oceans apart. In education, for example, there is a universal concern for growing class sizes, diminishing resources, falling standards of literacy and numeracy, and in several places a developing culture of violence or disruptive behaviour in schools. In health there are similar battles for resources and debates over priorities in their allocation. How the less advantaged members of society access health services and are supported by the welfare safety net is a constant thorn in the flesh of politicians and administrators around the globe.

One answer offered by most government administrations, an answer that is becoming less and less palatable from Washington to Wellington, is better management, or (as its critics would claim) galloping bureaucratization. In the words of sociologist David Lyon, "managerialism reigns" wherever pain is being experienced in government administration and economic direction. Lyon writes: "Increasingly, technique takes over... Questions of purposes in education, life and death in medicine, and social goals in politics are reduced to performance criteria: 'can we manage?' is the main question."[1]

Another contemporary writer, Philip Sampson, observes: "Of course market forces demand efficient and effective organizational contexts, and this in turn requires a new generation of managers who become the competent authorities to resolve the problem. The consequent growth in management services in Britain [and New Zealand] has been meteoric."[2] In New Zealand as elsewhere, this has also been parallelled by a phenomenal expansion of tertiary level degree courses in business studies.

But where all citizens without exception begin to feel the pain of living in our sophisticated and technically developed Western societies is in the area of community safety, and the vulnerability experienced by the ordinary man or woman in the face of violence. This violence can take the form either of loss of personal property through theft and burglary, or of injury to one's own person on city streets. 'Road rage' is a new expression of this threat. One growth industry common across the face of the Western world has been the marketing of home security and protection for vehicles and possessions. In New Zealand the number of private security firms has nearly doubled in a decade. Many people feel powerless in the face of such dangers. Children especially are at risk. Yet two World Wars, with the loss of hundreds of thousands of lives, were ostensibly waged in order to achieve the freedom and hope of living in peace and security.

There is also a restless spirit in politics. In New Zealand support for introducing a form of proportional representation into parliamentary elections has been as much a plea for a new era of politics, devoid of acrimony and offering greater accountability, as it is an informed preference for this particular model of government. It is as though voters were saying: "Something is not working; what we have had is no longer appropriate for the world we are in today. There have to be changes."

For a country like New Zealand, which for long had prided herself on being 'God's own' – clean, green, and uncrowded – it has also come as a shock to learn that this pleasant land is the nation with some of the highest rates of youth suicide in the industrialised West. People are asking: "What has gone wrong?"

A 1997 survey of teenagers reported that one in four young New Zealanders had attempted or contemplated suicide.[3] A Government discussion document on youth suicide, released in August, 1997, revealed that the New Zealand male youth suicide rate was 44.1 per 100,000, and female youth suicides 12.8. Compared with other OECD countries, this was the second-highest rate among young males, surpassed only by Finland, and the highest in the world for females. Between 1984 and 95 the annual number of youth suicides had risen from 72 deaths per annum to 156.[4] "What has gone wrong for this to happen in such a fair and pleasant land?" people were asking.

But this was not the only indicator that something was drastically awry. Another survey result issued that same month showed that "more than a quarter of teenagers between the ages of 14 and 18 are heavy drinkers."[5] One overseas observer commented that people "would never understand the reason for suicide unless they asked: 'What happened in this country during the last 30 years that made young people feel so alienated from their families, be more depressed, deliberately harm themselves and use drugs and alcohol more often ?'" He went on to express the opinion that economic reforms had left as their residue a generation who were "spiritually anorexic and morally ill. We have failed spectacularly to transmit a sense of meaning, purpose and belonging."[6]

Alienation occurs when any social order is convulsed by change too great or too deep to be assimilated, and dislocation is experienced. David Wells writes: "Unhitched from the old certainties, the modern person drifts within a society that is largely experienced as inhospitable...That is why managers and psychologists are so admired: they are controllers. Managers control the external world and psychologists control the internal world. Both offer results through technique rather than character..."[7]

Some relate this to an escalating loss of respect for authority and traditional institutions (police, teachers, clergy, politicians). The effect of this, they argue, has been to remove much of the supportive scaffolding that formerly helped bind communities together. In times past these respected social structures and hierarchies offered a publicly accepted framework within which one's freedom could be worked out. The boundaries to living in society were more clearly marked out in such an environment.

Yet this kind of development is not peculiar to New Zealand. It is a trend occurring in many parts of the Western world. Also, family breakdown appears to be no greater in this country than elsewhere. Why then should it lead to such depths of despair among the more vulnerable young people? Pain is accompanied by bewilderment.

The Pain of the Church

The Church has not escaped these pains. Hurting points, particularly for mainline Churches in the West, are several.

For older people with longer memories there is today the marked loss of status and influence of the Church in wider society. Some sociologists observe this as a consequence of the loss, through the process of secularization, of a particular plausibility structure that once gave the Church an assured position of privilege and esteem throughout the West.

A 'plausibility structure' describes an environment of credibility, e.g., for religious belief. This exists as an unspoken assumption of what is real and important to a certain culture. Such assumptions are usually developed over many generations, and provide a way of looking at the world that is taken for granted in that culture. It is supported by social organization, community celebrations, and public attitudes. In this case, the reference is to a plausibility structure that in the past provided a receptive climate for the Christian story. But the inroads of secularization and the advent of modernity have dismantled much of that structure. In his book *Telling the*

Story, Andrew Walker claims that "Christianity will have no future unless we build a new plausibility structure to nurture and sustain Christian commitment." [8]

Others explain what has happened as the disappearance of the 'sacred canopy' that once held Europe and its civilization together in a common 'Christian' bond, however different the nationalities, ethnic origins, languages or loyalties of its various peoples. In premodern societies religion often acted as an overarching umbrella, giving shelter and protection to their value-systems and traditions.

But commencing in the religiously desolate decade of the 1960s, a steady decline in membership of the traditional Churches began. Although this seemed to be bottoming out in the middle years of the 1990s, over all this represented a complete generation of decline. In New Zealand, for example, quite apart from a diminishing number of participating church members, there was also at each five year count a declining proportion of the largest single Christian grouping, 'census Anglicans', parallelled by a consistently rising number of people who simply 'objected to state' any religious affiliation or belief.

Whereas before 1960 those who would not identify with any religious grouping represented a mere 3 to 6 percent of the total population at most, as a body by the mid-1990s they significantly exceeded the number who put themselves down as Anglicans. In the 1996 census Anglican Christians comprised 17.46 percent of the total population or 631,000 people (a decrease of 13.7 percent since the previous census). But in this same 1996 census the number of those who chose 'no religion' came to 867,000 while those who 'objected to state' any religious affiliation amounted to a further 256,000 of the population, a total of 1.1 million people. By the end of the 20th century therefore, a third of the total New Zealand population were no longer prepared to identify themselves as Christians.

Many people complain about the traditional Churches' lack of appeal to the younger generation. At one stage this group was known as the baby boomers, children of the post-war period. In the 1990s their age group was also referred to as 'Generation X'.

Generation X

A young Australian, Tim Corney, writes about his age-group:

"I belong to Generation X – the children of the most divorced, most mobile parents this century. I live in a time of exceptionally high incidence of youth suicide and drug-induced road trauma, of child abuse and violent crime. Hope, for my generation has gone missing...The result is that I no longer know who or what I am supposed to be. Gender distinctions have been blurred; national cultures appropriated and dismantled, normative values have been stood on their head and institutions ridiculed and maligned. Societies, structures and functions are breaking down... Hope epitomises the difference between then and now. The 1970s brimmed with hope; the 1990s do not. The hope that was promised was not delivered and cynicism, sarcasm, meaninglessness and irony have filled the void.

"As I walk the streets of my city, the spray-can voices shout out in polychrome unison the disillusionment, boredom and helplessness of a street culture that has stopped trying to make sense of the world. [Helmut] Thielicke said, 'The Gospel must continuously be forwarded to a new address because the recipient is continually changing his place of residence'. The current address for the average young person is as far from the Church as the East is from the West. The Church does not even have the technology to mail the Gospel on, let alone know how to package it."[9]

Baby-boomers both inside and outside the Church, according to culture observer David Wells, share two similar traits. First, they have a hunger for religious experience along with aversion to theological expression of that experience, and a hunger for God but disenchantment with dogma or doctrine. This does not draw them by preference to traditional Christianity. Secondly, they are distinguished by an inclination to dispense with boundaries, and so have no problem with 'shopping around' for the Church that suits them. This results in creating for this generation a spiritual smorgasbord for which the only criterion of truth is the pragmatic and personal one: Does it work for me?[10]

By the 1990s these baby-boomers were now themselves becoming parents of teenagers. Unless finding themselves in a strong Christian family setting, or introduced to the faith by some of their own peers who were Christians, this new generation were also not being drawn to the Church or assimilating a modicum of faith from the wider community.

The situation has not been helped by the new climate of religious pluralism, not just as a descriptive fact of life in the late 20th century, but as a prescriptive public policy, promoted by Western state and civic authorities.[11] Such a policy declines to give greater status to any one faith over another, even if (as in the case of the Christian faith) one religion has been the historic shaper of the majority culture in that land. In effect this declares to all that the truth of religion is not really a matter of public concern. It belongs to the private areas of life. In appearing to be even-handed, such a policy in fact makes a strong statement about the *un*importance of religious faith of *any* kind in public life.

In part this is an outcome of secularization, the result of an increasingly secular spirit pervading all Western societies, some more than others. Leander Keck describes secularization as "a process in which a growing number of people find a religious sensibility irrelevant for their own thought and conduct, and basically harmless (though perhaps emotionally useful) for those who retain it, but who feel threatened when this sensibility 'goes public'."[12]

In New Zealand this is more pronounced than in Great Britain. In Britain, for example, the Churches are constantly in the news, and the views of church leaders are given weight both as news items and also in the editorials of major papers. In the British quality papers, hardly a day goes by without at least one major piece of news involving the Church or some other aspect of religion in the land. This is often a sympathetic portrayal (unless, deservedly, one of the denominations makes a fool of itself in some way).

Each morning there is an extended *Thought for the Day*, with prayer, on BBC Radio One. Hymns are heard more often; people talk about faith more

Religious Pluralism

The pluralist society developed as a response to changed social conditions during the 19th and 20th centuries. First, increased *urbanization* brought disparate peoples into close proximity, with a need to learn to live together with their differences; secondly, much greater *mobility* of populations exposed more people to diverse cultures and belief systems that had to be related to their own in ways that made good sense; thirdly, advances in *mass media communications* compressed time and space for entire populations, even for those who remained rural people or who did not travel, and this required an adjustment of traditional thinking to accommodate this enlarged and enriched world that they were now encountering.

This sociological change has been a challenge to the Christian faith, particularly where it has for long served as the 'sacred canopy' of a society. Two quite different responses from within the Christian fold have been, on the one hand to advocate religious pluralism, which in the end denies the possibility of our own or another's beliefs being true and determinative for all (the liberal answer); and on the other hand to assert the truth of Christian conviction without due consideration of other beliefs (the conservative answer). One pressing task for the Church in the West, in societies that can only become even more pluralistic under postmodernity, is to discover a path that respects other faiths, yet remains true to its own.

openly; political leaders are able to be quizzed about their deepest beliefs.

Contrast this with a country such as New Zealand where any media coverage of the Churches or their beliefs is likely to be slight, superficial, and more often than not controversial. In 1997 religious programming on New Zealand public radio was reduced to one repeated Sunday slot, with a format that came across more like a Polytech introduction to a course on the world's religions than an act of Christian worship or an attempt to reflect on issues of the day and the life of the nation from a Christian perspective.

Radio New Zealand (RNZ) cut back the total weekly programming on National Radio from 140 to 100 minutes per week. Compare with this the BBC allocation of almost 300 minutes per week. The RNZ content consisted of 30 minutes of Christian hymns, a maximum five minutes of every kind of religious news from around the world, and up to 20 minutes of questions put to a 'resident expert' who could be an adherent of any religion. The Christian 'expert' called upon was frequently a liberal theologian who, on the first such programme, openly stated his position that all religions were purely human constructs created as an endeavour of different cultures and times to answer the deep questions of life and its meaning. Only weeks before the new programme was introduced, this religious studies academic had publicly promoted a view that the divinity of Christ was a creation of the early Church to bolster its flagging fortunes, the Gospel accounts of the birth of Jesus a fabrication, and Christmas a human invention.

To many this new arrangement of religious broadcasting seemed a deliberate secular rebuff to the religious sensibilities of the nation, neither fair in its allocation of time measured alongside the census figures of declared religious conviction in New Zealand, nor just in its representation of the Christian proportion of this conviction.

The end impression conveyed by much of the media in New Zealand is that religious faith – including the Christian Church – is incidental to public life and largely irrelevant to modern living.

Modern Idols

Not that Western people are entirely without popular idols of some sort at the end of the 20th century. But, more often than Christians like to acknowledge, it is the gods of consumerism or scientism that are most likely to be held up as the idols for this generation to look to for their salvation.

Back in the 16th century John Calvin had said: "The human heart is a factory of idols." Contemporary writers on this theme identify a variety of different idols that attract the devotion of people in modern societies.[13] Brian Walsh names as destructive idols of Western societies in this day "three good dimensions of creation [that] have been absolutized...These three idols are *scientism* (the belief that science provides us with authoritative knowledge and functions as the omniscient source of revelation in our culture), *technicism* (the effective translation of scientific knowledge into power and control of the creation which promises us a scientific-technical omnipotence), and *economism* (the golden head of the idol that believes that a rising standard of living is the ultimate goal in life and the only route to personal happiness and societal harmony)." Walsh then proceeds to demonstrate the inadequacy and emptiness of these alternative idols.[14]

It is widely accepted that there is now throughout Western societies a 'culture of consumption' as against the mere consuming of the increasing variety of goods available through increased production.[15] 'Consumerism' entails both the creation of desire and imagined need and also the experience of sampling or purchasing goods. This experience is the pleasure to be derived from the exercise, as much through the stimulation of all the senses which modern shopping malls provide in the process of viewing, as in the acquisition of needed items. 'Retail therapy', some would describe it. Others would go as far as claiming that for many the Mall has become the temple visited weekly for relief from the pain of life in the suburbs or work in the office, even if such shopping complexes are transparently temples to mammon.

"Those who make idols grow to be like them;
and so do all who put their trust in them."

Psalm 115: 8, *A New Zealand Prayer Book*

Consumerism, then, is the pursuit of goods as much 'for the experience of the chase' as to meet genuine needs. *Scientism* on the other hand is the elevation of science beyond its due limits of authority, investing it with powers and hopes it can never fulfil. Together they characterize the spirit of modernity. Bryan Appleyard describes modernity as: "the story of a culture, our culture, being progressively overwhelmed and transformed by science... Religion had been defeated. Western society would, henceforth, be secular. The sheer energy, power and effectiveness of science had weakened the old

The New Megachurches

The emergence of megachurches may be in part explained by the influence of the baby-boomer generation (to whom such Churches especially appeal) whose expectations have been shaped by modernity with its emphasis on infotainment, self-therapy, and bounty of choice without any accompanying commitment. Alongside this fare, small struggling neighbourhood one-dimensional Churches with limited resources may well appear unattractive, uninviting, and too fraught with the prospect of personal involvement, however real and faithful their worship may be. "This generation is used to working and living within large bureaucratic structures, so they may feel more at home in the corporate environs of a Megachurch than in the more familial context of a small congregation."[16]

faith until it had become just one more voice among other things, merely an opinion. It may have answered questions that science did not, but the source of its answers was no longer believed, so neither were its answers."[17]

The mainline Churches in some countries have a further painful reminder of what they once were and where they once stood in the community. This is in the proliferation of 'culturally specific new Churches', that is, Churches that appeal to a particular section of society or to a sub-culture within a community, e.g., the baby-boomers. Sometimes these are located uncomfortably close to one of the older Churches, and almost certainly have among their key leaders and membership a number of former, dissident members of those traditional Churches. Living and working alongside such new Churches, with their often booming congregations, can be a pain not readily spoken of openly, yet often deeply felt by some mainline church leaders, only too aware of how ill-equipped they feel themselves to be to compete with these other more charismatic ministries represented in the Pentecostal bodies.

"The Pentecostal movement", writes Harvey Cox, "provides us with an invaluable set of clues, not just about the wider religious upsurge but about an even more comprehensive set of changes. These changes are not just religious ones, they add up to a basic cultural shift for which the overtly spiritual dimension is not just the tip of the iceberg but the stream in which the iceberg is floating. A major refiguration of our most fundamental attitudes and patterns, one that will ultimately alter not just the way some people think but the ways we all think, feel, work and govern."[18]

In the wider community there is another pain not known before in the way it is today – awareness of a diminishing respect for the sacred, especially in the cities and towns. In Britain, the Archbishop of Canterbury, George Carey, told a congregation in November, 1996: "Church of England clergy are having a tougher time than ever before. They face a culture of contempt and deep cynicism." He went on to speak of how today "ministry in [Great Britain] was harder than it ever was."

In New Zealand with each passing year more and more churches are having to be locked for longer and longer periods of the day; some even on Sundays outside of worship times. Those that are brave enough to remain open often see items of value being removed or desecrated. Vandalism increases with affluence. Insurance charges keep in step. War memorials share the same fate. School classrooms and public utilities fare no better. "What have we done to deserve this?" ask the older generation. Those who are younger presume it has always been like this.

Yet it is also true to say that there are many Churches, both new independent fellowships and mainline Churches, who take the challenge of these changing times seriously and seek to tackle the godlessness they find about them in their secular communities. But here they encounter a further point of pain – uncertainty as to what are appropriate ways of evangelism in their contemporary world. Reading the times aright proves baffling. Old ways do not seem to work. New ways have limited success, which then have to be supplemented by even newer and better techniques. One imported parish life programme is succeeded by the next. 'Church Growth' has become an ecclesiastical industry, with professional consultants, but without obvious signs of the tides of paganism being turned, despite Christian Canutes who

Culture

'Culture' is that pattern of unspoken assumptions and commonly held values that provides parameters for a community's behaviour. Culture establishes what is acceptable and what is unacceptable (at least as a public front) within that group of people.

Culture is seldom taught; it is mostly caught. Within a larger society there may be a number of sub-cultures, each with its own inner set of behaviour patterns and expectations, yet related to and taking account – positively or negatively – of the culture of the wider society of which it is part. (After all, a 'cult' on the surface looks very much like a truncated portion of a 'culture'!)

Nelson Mandela writes in his autobiography: "My life, and that of most Xhosas at the time, was shaped by custom, ritual and taboo. This was the alpha and omega of our existence, and went unquestioned. Men followed the path laid out for them by their fathers; women led the same lives as their mothers before them. Without being told, I soon assimilated the elaborate rules that governed the relations between men and women."[19]

give assurances that 'revival is at hand'. Pervading all, when honesty comes to the surface, there is a widespread feeling that 'the Church' (particularly in its traditional structures and inherited ministry patterns) is ill-equipped for these times and circumstances.

Whatever the specific indicators we individually encounter and take notice of, there is enough evidence on hand to convince many people that, like hidden movements of the Pacific plate miles beneath the earth's crust, Western culture is undergoing deep changes in the final decades of the 20th century. The questions are: What is happening? Why is this so? Where is it leading? What can we do about it – particularly as Christian Churches? What is our calling and mission as Churches in such a new environment?

A Silent Revolution

Many are coming to recognise that Western civilization is experiencing a revolution as significant as the 16th century Protestant Reformation, but this time bloodless, and without fanfare or victory parades. Many describe this as a 'paradigm shift', a complete change in the ordering of society and in the fundamental ways in which we understand our world. Alvin Toffler writes of this as a "hinge of history". Mikhail Gorbachev offers a similar observation: "Humankind stands at a watershed in its history."[20] We underestimate the seriousness of this crisis in Western culture at our own peril.

Yet this is questioned by others who see any changes taking place as no greater than previous generations have experienced over the centuries, a situation requiring no more than the response of a fine tuning of Church or society. This has always been the case in the past, they argue. What we are going through is no more than the growing pains of change and development. And in universal human experience, growth spurts in adolescence have usually involved some measure of pain. One commentator has expressed this ambivalence in this way: "There is a widely shared sense that Western ways of seeing, knowing and representing have irreversibly altered in recent times; but there is little consensus over what this might mean or what direction Western culture is now taking. Has modernity really come to a close, or has it simply undergone a change of appearance?"[21]

An intermediate position may be that suggested by A. Huyssens: "What appears on one level as the latest fad, advertising pitch and hollow spectacle is part of a slowly emerging transformation in Western societies, a change in sensibility for which the term 'postmodern' is actually, at least for now, wholly adequate...I don't want to be misunderstood as claiming that there is a whole-sale paradigm shift of the cultural, social and economic orders; any such claim would be overblown. But in an important sector of our culture there is a noticeable shift in sensibility, practices and discourse formations which distinguishes a postmodern set of assumptions, experiences and propositions from that of a preceding period."[22]

How, then, do those who see signs of a major Western cultural shift of unprecedented proportions read the situation at the end of the 20th century?

Witnesses to Culture Shift

"Our society is in the throes of a monumental transition, moving from modernity to postmodernity...The transition from the modern era to the postmodern era poses a grave challenge to the church in its mission to its own next generation...To reach people in the new postmodern context, we must set ourselves to the task of deciphering the implications of postmodernism for the Gospel."[23]

Stanley Grenz

"As the 20th century progressed, large blocks of people became increasingly sceptical about inherited religious dogma, and ecclesiastical institutions steadily lost their power to shape cultures...But something else was happening as well. Not only were large numbers of people becoming alienated from traditional religion, they were also losing confidence in the bright promises of science and progress."[24]

Harvey Cox

"Quite unprecedented social and cultural shifts are occurring...that fundamentally question the whole edifice of modernity."[25]

David Lyon

"Western culture is in the middle of a fundamental transformation: a 'shape of life' is growing old. The demise of the old is being hastened by the end of colonialism, the uprising of women, the revolt of other cultures against white Western hegemony, shifts in the balance of economic and political power within the world economy, and a growing awareness of the costs as well as the benefits of scientific and technological 'progress'."[26]

Jane Flax

"As we approach the end of the 20th century, modernity is in radical decline. Its legitimating myths are no longer believed with any conviction."[27]

Middleton and Walsh

"What has unfolded in theological and missionary circles during the last two decades is the result of a fundamental paradigm shift, not only in mission or theology, but in the experience and thinking of the whole world. Many of us are only aware of the crisis we are facing now...what is happening in our time is not the first paradigm shift the world (or the church) has experienced. There have been profound crises and paradigm shifts before. Each of them has constituted the end of one world and the birth of another, in which much of what people used to do and think had to be redefined."[28]

David Bosch

"...the evidence...reveals in the closing decades of the 20th century a critical moment in the religious history of [Great Britain], and one which we would do well to ponder. They are decades in which both traditional institutions and traditional certainties struggle, in secular as well as religious life."[29]

Grace Davie

"The truth is that we are in a time of transition, an in-between period when the old is dying and the new has yet to be born. The values, assumptions and structures that have governed us for so long have come to their logical end, and now we find ourselves at a dead end. But new values, patterns and institutions have not yet emerged. We are caught in the middle, stranded between paradigms."[30]

Jim Wallis

As Diogenes Allen, for example, puts it: "A massive intellectual revolution is taking place that is perhaps as great as that which marked off the modern world from the Middle Ages. The foundations of the modern world are collapsing, and we are entering a postmodern world. The principles forged during the Enlightenment...are crumbling."[31]

This book sees the current degree of change as a critical reshaping of Western culture that is taking place with serious consequences for both the Church and society in the Western world.

"There has been a sea-change in cultural as well as in political-economic practices since around 1972. This sea-change is bound up with the emergence of new dominant ways in which we experience space and time."[32]

David Harvey

What makes others sceptical about such dramatic claims? It all depends on how the signs are read and interpreted. But against such scepticism, there is an impressive coincidence of evidence of deep change discernible in quite different fields of human endeavour and interest. When these are found to be saying much the same there is an accumulating weight of argument for the validity of such claims. And connecting threads of response are to be discerned in disciplines as diffuse as architecture, literature, the arts, philosophy, pop culture, and fashion.

In the end, does it matter? As Christians, are not the lines already clearly enough drawn and our divine commission adequately spelled out for us, whatever the changing nature of society about us? What difference, then, does it really make?

The Incarnation tells us that Christ came to the world as it was at a particular time. He took upon himself the garb and customs of that day and place. He knew and entered into the culture of his age with the Gospel of the Kingdom of God.

When the Apostle Paul moved out of the Jewish-dominated areas of Judea and Asia Minor and brought the Gospel to Athens, he recognized he was in another world, needing to address people at a different place in their relationship to God. So he adapted his ministry and message accordingly.

As the world enters a new millennium, Christian Churches in the West are also now no longer in Jerusalem, but in Athens. Christians need to understand this changed world they now live in, so different from the world their Churches grew accustomed to and comfortable within over the previous millennium. This book seeks to describe this new world of the West, and how Christian Churches, along with many other institutions of society, may need to change – considerably – in order to take their place with confidence and hope in a new century and a new millennium.

Modernity and Postmodernity

In brief, *Moving Between Times* will argue that all of Western society, together with those other areas of the world that are significantly shaped and affected by Western ways, is in transition between an era of *modernity* and a new way of thinking, looking at our world, and living together, presently designated *postmodernity*. Middleton and Walsh express the change in this way: "We live in a time of cultural transition, where we are experiencing the continuance – even heightening – of central features of modernity, side by side with genuinely novel, postmodern elements."[33]

The period of *modernity* stretched from approximately the 18th century to the 20th century, but has only just come to its fullest fruition and flowering in 'high modernity' during the final decades of the 20th century.

Postmodernity is still emerging. We cannot describe it with confident precision, because we are part of it, and because it is still taking shape. But the emergence of postmodernity since the mid-20th century has repercussions of the greatest significance for the whole of society, not least the Christian Church.

GLOSSARY

- **Modernity** indicates the *period* we have been living in, particularly in a heightened form through the 20th century. Modernity can be seen as an outcome of the 18th century intellectual Enlightenment together with the impact of various other social and political revolutions that followed over the next two centuries, culminating in the vast changes to our way of living brought about by advances in technology during the 20th century.

  Sometimes reference is also made to the period *before* the Enlightenment as being 'premodern'. J. Bottum writes: "...these words premodern, modern, and postmodern are too slippery to mean much. Taken to refer to the history of ideas they seem to name the periods before, during, and after the Enlightenment; but taken to refer to the history of events, they seem to name the period from creation to the rise of science, the period from the rise of science until World War II, and the period since the war. ...Perhaps, though definitions based on intent are always weak, the best definition nevertheless involves intent: it is premodern to seek beyond rational knowledge for God; it is modern to desire to hold knowledge in the structure of human rationality (with or without God); it is postmodern to see the impossibility of such knowledge."[34]

- **Modernization** is the *process* of becoming a modern society, according to Western precepts and ideals. It involves such disparate dynamics as social organization, industrialization, the information explosion, technological advances, philosophical ideas.

- **Modernism** is the *application* in various fields of human interest, e.g., the arts, of the ideas and outlook nourished by modernity. "Modernism is a troubled and fluctuating response to conditions of modernity produced by a particular process of modernization."[35]

- **Postmodernity** describes the *new era* we appear to be entering, an era that retains some but rejects others of the features of modernity.

"Modernity is the intellectual and cultural heritage of the Enlightenment project – namely, the rejection of traditional and religious sources of authority in favour of reason and knowledge as the road to human emancipation...Postmodernity refers to the progressive loss of confidence in, if not failure of, the Enlightenment project since 1945. This accelerated in the seventies and eighties as the consequences of modernization became more apparent."[36]

During this extended period of transition, both modernity and postmodernity coexist. "Two accounts, one of the emergence of postmodernism out of modernism, the other of the emergence of postmodernity out of modernity, run on adjoining tracks, sometimes crossing, but also sometimes diverging from each other in significant ways."[37] This confuses the scene for the observer of society, and adds to the bewilderment and pain of the ordinary citizen.

- **Postmodernism** is the *expression* of the ideas and values of postmodernity in different areas of life. Some evidence of postmodernism has been discernible, for example, in pop culture, architecture and the arts, since the 1980s. "Postmodernism is the very loose term used to describe the new aesthetic, cultural and intellectual forms and practices which are emerging in the 1980s and 1990s. As the word suggests, 'postmodernism' follows, and is rapidly replacing, modernism, the term used to describe the cultural styles and movements of the first half of the 20th century...Now a new, more populist culture is emerging, closer to everyday life, to the market place, to consumption, and to the new popular culture of the media – a culture which renounces purity, mastery of form and elitism and is more playful, ironic, and eclectic in style."[38]

The Course and
Character of Modernity

The Era of Modernity, 1789-1989

"A story of two walls, and what happened in between," is the graphic way Thomas Oden describes the era of modernity in its quest for a rationalized world.[1] The first wall to fall was that of the Bastille in 1789; the second, the Berlin Wall in 1989. Although intimations of modernity were present well before the French Revolution, this was the period when modernity projected itself on to the public arena with vigour. Today modernity still very much shapes our world and affects our everyday lives, even well after the ending of the Communist regime in Eastern Europe. But there is also an awareness that modernity is now a lame duck, and that its days are numbered.

Eras such as this do not normally come and go with such suddenness and precision, or with so convenient a brace of images. They linger and overlap, sometimes across several generations. However, as Andrew Walker comments, "Oden's French Revolutionary origination of modernity does serve one very useful purpose. It is not until that time that we can say that modernity 'hit the streets' and entered the public domain – political, social and economic. Until that time, the modernization programme of the new cultural era had been little more than the gossip of the great houses and salons of the European aristocracy, and the more philosophical concern of its intellectual elite."[2]

The fall of the Bastille can be viewed as a symbol of the open onslaught of modernity on the aristocratic authorities and hierarchical structures of Europe's feudal or premodern past; the collapse of the Berlin Wall, on the other hand, symbolized the end of a different form of hierarchy and exercise of power – that of bureaucratic state socialism, a classic expression of the functional rationalism that was a prime feature of modernity at its apex.

Origins in the Renaissance

Modernity emerged as the confluence of several different streams over a period of two to three centuries. Indeed, one could say that the full current and flow of the river of modernity was not really experienced until all the various contributory streams came together in the second half of the 20th century. This was not long before the accumulated torrent of modernity finally spent its force and merged into the restless ocean of postmodernity.

The springs of modernity can be traced initially to the liberating effects of the 15th century Renaissance, when the first Christian humanism stirred and cautiously placed 'Man' at the centre of reality and of all that mattered most. In effect this served to undercut the cultural dominance of the Church in the West, and the medieval worldview that went with the Church. Renaissance thinkers rekindled interest in the physical world as an object of study in its own right, and laid down principles of study and observation that would form the future platform for modern science. The key figure here was Francis Bacon (1561-1626).

In the end, Bacon died as an outcome of his most famous scientific experiment. Neil Postman describes how "he and his good friend Dr Wither-bone were taking a coach ride on a wintry day when, seeing snow on the ground, Bacon wondered if flesh might not be preserved in snow, as it is in salt. The two decided to find out at once. They bought a hen, removed its innards, and stuffed the body with snow. Poor Bacon never learned the result of his experiment, because he fell immediately ill from the cold, most probably with bronchitis, and died three days later."[3]

Francis Bacon

Francis Bacon (1561-1626) at the time of the Renaissance promoted a vision of humans exercising power over nature by means of the discovery of nature's secrets. This gave initial impetus to the way of thinking that would culminate in what we now call modernity. But also he stood at the threshold of the Age of Reason. In a sense therefore Francis Bacon marks the transition from the Renaissance to the Enlightenment. In his posthumously published book, *The New Atlantis*, Bacon described the ideal society. Above all, in this society people would look to science as providing the key to happiness. His famous dictum was "knowledge is power" – because it offers the ability to alter our circumstances so they conform to our desires. Bacon's vision laid the foundation for modern technological societies. He is considered the father of modern science.

The Enlightenment

A further major contributory stream to the evolution of modernity, and probably the single most significant influence on the form modernity was to continue to take right up until the end of the 20th century, was the revolution in ways of thought and understanding known as The Enlightenment. Subsequently the period this introduced came also to be known as 'The Age of Reason', the critical mark of this time being the priority given to reason as the means of both discovering and mastering the natural world.

The convictions and goals of the Enlightenment, sometimes referred to as 'the Enlightenment project', were based on the confidence that knowledge is certain, objective and good.[4]

- That knowledge is CERTAIN required a reliable method of demonstrating the essential correctness of philosophic, scientific, religious, moral, and political doctrines. The method the philosophers of the Enlightenment devised involved an absolute faith in humanity's rational capabilities.
- That knowledge is OBJECTIVE required the modernist to claim access to dispassionate knowledge, that is, to be able to view the world as (they

sincerely believed) impartial observers. This also led to the specialization of knowledge through division of the scientific endeavour into separate disciplines.

- That knowledge is GOOD assumed that the pursuit and discovery of knowledge is always to be commended. This lent an optimistic attitude to the Enlightenment efforts. It also led to the belief that progress is inevitable, and that science coupled with the power of education will eventually free us from our vulnerability to nature, as well as from all social bondage.

All this in turn hinged on human freedom. So all beliefs that seem to curtail autonomy, or to be based on some external authority other than reason, became suspect. (But 'freedom' could be interpreted in different ways. Under modernity, freedom *of* religion eventually became corrupted into freedom *from* religion!)

"The modern world turned out to be Newton's mechanistic universe populated by Descartes' autonomous, rational substance. In such a world, theology was forced to give place to the natural sciences, and the central role formerly enjoyed by the theologian became the pre-rogative of the natural scientist."[5]

Stanley Grenz

The premodern, medieval world of Western Europe was overturned in a profound series of intellectual, religious, philosophical, social and political revolutions stretching over the last five centuries, but only achieving the fullest flowering of modernity in the final four decades of the 20th century. Anthony Giddens says we cannot overestimate the profundity of these changes, even compared with the current impact of postmodernity. He writes: "The modes of life brought into being by modernity have swept us away from *all* traditional types of social order, in quite unprecedented fashion. In both their extensionality and in their intentionality the transformations involved in modernity are more profound than most sorts of change

34

Key Figures of the Age of Reason

René Descartes (1596-1650) laid the philosophical foundation for the modern edifice with his focus on doubt, which led him to conclude that the existence of the thinking self is the first truth that doubt cannot deny (*cogito ergo sum – I think, therefore I am*). He argued that the reasoning subject, rather than divine revelation, is the only sure starting point for knowledge and reflection. His arguments have convinced even many modern theologians. Hence the influence of rationalistic philosophy on theology no less than on other disciplines during the period of modernity.

Isaac Newton (1642-1727) pictured the physical world as a grand, orderly machine, the laws and regularity of which could be discerned by the human mind. Newton's goal was to explain the workings of this universe. A Christian, he still wanted to be able to show how "the heavens declare the glory of God". The modern human can appropriately be characterized as Descartes' autonomous, rational substance encountering Newton's mechanistic world.

John Locke (1632-1704). As the Age of Reason unfolded, revealed religion increasingly came under attack, and natural religion (respect for the observable physical world of nature, without the aid of revelation) increasingly gained the status of true religion. John Locke was crucial in this process. He advocated releasing Christianity from its dogmatic baggage so as to let it rest upon reason alone. This led to the development of *deism,* which effectively reduced religion to its most basic elements, and provided a God who was little more that the great Watchmaker, or the First Cause and Creator of the universe. Andrew Walker writes: "With the rise of Deism and Unitarianism in the 18th century, there was a wholesale attack upon classical theism. The gardens of the court at

Versailles in France and the landscapes of Capability Brown in England reflected a God of design and order rather than one of personal revel- ation."[6]

Immanuel Kant (1724-1804) stands at the end of the Age of Reason, yet his reformulation of the ideals of the Age of Reason breathed new life into the Enlightenment project and gave it the shape that would mark the late modern era. His work signified the inauguration of modernity in its fullness. His contribution was to elevate the autonomous self to the centre of the philosophical agenda.

The Christian Astronomers "Copernicus, Kepler and Galileo put in place the dynamite that would blow up the theology and metaphysics of the medieval world. Newton lit the fuse. In the ensuing explosion...Scripture lost most of its authority. Theology, once Queen of the Sciences, was now reduced to the status of Court Jester. Worst of all, the meaning of existence itself became an open question."[7]

characteristic of prior periods. On the extensional plane they have served to establish forms of social interconnection which span the globe; in intentional terms they have come to alter some of the most intimate and personal features of our day-to-day existence."[8]

The steps to modernity

In outline, the successive stages involved in the emergence of modernity into full maturity were these:

1. The *Renaissance*, reinstating 'Man' at centre of the universe (in the 15th century)
2. The *Reformation*, (in the 16th century), rejecting the centralised author- itarian dominance of the medieval Church that had undergirded feudal social hierarchies.

3. The *Enlightenment*, elevating reason over revelation as the way to real understanding and true knowledge (in the 17th to 18th centuries).

4. The *French Revolution* (and similar later uprisings), overthrowing the power of aristocratic class structures, and empowering the under-privileged (from the end of the 18th century on).

5. The *Industrial Revolution*, revealing the potential of the creative and managerial powers of man in reordering society according to human design (through the 18th and 19th centuries). "If the French Revolution gave to modernity its characteristic form and consciousness – revolution based on reason – the Industrial Revolution provided it with its material substance...It was only with the British Industrial Revolution of the late 18th century that modernity reached its material form. Partly this is because of the very explosiveness of the development – a speeding up of economic evolution to the point where it took on revolutionary proportions."[9]

6. The *Technological Revolution* (20th century), placing the fruits of advanced discoveries in the hands of ordinary people at affordable prices.

7. The *Information Explosion* (late 20th century), from the advent of the microchip in 1971, providing easy access to all that is known, to everyone who seeks it – instantly.

Over a total period of 500 years then, modernity has gradually, but with increasing momentum, become a global culture that few can resist. In 1996 an editorial in a leading paper wrote of "a sense of powerlessness against the international forces of modernity."[10] Over this time, the world of monarchs and monasteries has been transformed into a world of cellphones and credit cards. The divine right of kings has become the divine right to things.

Features of Modernity

What have been the outcomes of these last two centuries of steadily maturing modernity? How do they affect our world in practical ways today? Why has the Enlightenment project collapsed, and what was wrong with modernity to provoke the response of postmodernity?

The principle features of modernity that today continue to influence our public life as Western nations, and our private lives as citizens within these nations, are threefold:

*The obsession of modernity with **rationality*** – not just adequate provision for the place of reason in public and personal life, but an insistence that finally all we believe and do and value must be tried at the ultimate bar of rationality. It is the Enlightenment emphasis on the liberating role of reason carried to excess.

As a tool of science, rationality opened the door to both the industrial and the technological revolutions. But applied to many other areas of life, it has crippled the imagination and impoverished the soul. In architecture it led to the sterility of many of the designs, commercial and residential, of the 1960s and 1970s, 'carbuncles' on the face of our cities, as the Prince of Wales has described some of these. In Biblical studies, for more than a century it had placed an intellectual straitjacket on the study of the Old Testament, diverted attention from the content to the context of the New Testament, and taken the mystery out of faith and the miracles out of the life of Jesus.

In reaction to this prime feature of modernity there has been a mounting feeling that the time had come to reduce free-ranging reason to size and return it both to the security of its proper partnership with faith and feeling, and to respect for God's revelation as a valid source of truth.

*The conviction of modernity about **progress*** – not just change, but the belief that things can only get better, and that there is an inevitability about progress. This conviction was boosted by Darwinian theories of evolution in the 19th century which, for all their insights into probable ways God creates life, were extrapolated to fit all manner of human and social development, and applied, for example, to philosophies of education, child rearing, and theological learning.

Enlightenment belief in progress was based on the conviction that, because the universe was both orderly and knowable, and therefore open to control, use of the proper methods under the benign guidance of reason would invariably lead to a better world. Enlightenment thinkers were convinced that not only was such progress possible, it was also within human grasp. In contrast, historians of the Age of Reason looked on the Middle

Modernity Described

The Iron Hammer of Modernity

"Modernity broke the shackles of tradition, religion and superstition with the hammer of a humanism forged in Greece and Rome. It was the Enlightenment which fused this humanism with Reason, and Kant's three Critiques have taken the pride of place in articulating this fusion as a modern vision. The experience of modernity, then, is to break with traditional hierarchies and justifications."[11]

The Emergence of Modernity

"Modernity emerges in embryonic form in the humanism of the Renaissance. It slowly develops with the individualism and freedom of the Reformation, and the rise of merchant banking in the 16th century. It matures in the philosophical Enlightenment of the 18th century, and becomes socially and economically inculturated in the 19th and 20th centuries. Approaching the third millennium, we can legitimately say that modernity has grown old but has not yet passed away."[12]

The Dynamics of Modernity

Modernization, writes David Wells, is "a process driven by four main realities:

1. *Capitalism* which has reorganised the social structure for the purposes of manufacturing, production, and consumption...concentrated the population into cities, and produced massive systems of finance, banking, law, communications and transportation. In short, it has changed the shape of our world, how we relate to it, where we live, how we experience our work, and the values and expectations that we bring with us in order to be adaptable to and successful in this public sphere.
2. *Technology* facilitates the processes of capitalism, and rationalizes all of life...People who live in technology-dominated societies are

prone to think naturalistically and to subject all of life to a calculus of benefits – to assume that what is most efficient is most ethical.

3. *Urbanization*...mass migrations of peoples...have brought with them their own ethnic identities, cultural habits, languages, religions and values – all of which have been brought into close proximity to one another [through urbanization]. The new multicultural environment has produced a secular ecumenism and a powerful demand for pluralism, for mutual tolerance, for private space in which to hold one's beliefs, live one's own lifestyle, do what one wants to do... producing an encompassing relativism as well.

4. *Telecommunication* has made us citizens of the global village. Television is perhaps less a window on the world than a surrogate eye pre-selecting what images of the world we will be exposed to."[13]

The Symbols of Modernity

"If the savings book was the epitome of modern life, the credit card is the paradigm of the postmodern one."[14]

Ages as an era of superstition and barbarism. Actual progress that was achieved, e.g., in the Industrial Revolution, led Enlightenment thinkers to ooze with optimism for the future, especially under the aegis and with the intervention of Western civilization. Utopia was within reach. Western civilization was Europe's gift to the world, especially, for example, to the uncivilized peoples of Africa.

It has taken two hideous world wars, the horrors of the holocaust, and a succession of heinous mass murders or group suicides in Great Britain, the United States, Tasmania and even New Zealand (e.g., the Aramoana massacre), to convince us that perhaps modernity had got this wrong. (Yet blind optimism still clouds the lenses of many Westerners in these same countries!)

The focus of modernity on **the individual**. This, too, was a feature from the beginning, when Christian humanists of the Renaissance first determined to put Man at the centre of their universe. Initially this was little more than an intellectual exercise, accompanied in those early centuries by a continuing belief that it was only under God that Man could be the proper focus of study and concern. But over time, and particularly in the last hundred years under the influence of secular ideas, the divine was steadily diminished as the context for such humanist studies, and then dispensed with altogether.

Parallel with that, during this century there has been exponential growth in pressure groups agitating for and legislation protecting the rights of the individual. Little, on the other hand, that stresses the value of community, or the duties which should be the accompaniment of citizenship, or the sacrifices each of us at times may need to make for the good of others. Again, a sense that the pendulum has swung too far in this direction for too long may well contribute to the often sharp reactions of postmodernity that Western societies are now beginning to experience.

Other features of modernity also need to be taken into account. One of these is its grand ideas of universality. In the field of architecture, under the universalizing conditions of modernity, the world traveller discovers that international air terminals around the globe often look more like one another than reflections of local culture and building styles; bedrooms in international hotels have little that tell you visually where you are when you awake bewildered after another leg of a tiring journey between continents. There is also modernity's captivity to concepts of dualism, and its supreme confidence in its own abilities to solve all problems in its own strength.

Modernity promised – and still threatens, in its decadent heyday – to become a world culture. This is a new phenomenon for the world. Formerly cultures were local, ethnic or religious, e.g., Judaism, Islam, Irish identity, Maoritanga. The culture of modernity, however, threatens to overcome and suborn all other cultures, imposing upon them its own more dominant shadow.

Postmodernity is in part a reaction against this possibility, an emphasis on the local rather than the universal, diversity rather than uniformity, difference rather than sameness, plurality rather than singularity.

We are cautioned that this 'world culture' should not simply be interpreted as a new, uniform global culture. "We sometimes fail to recognize this because we have confused the ubiquity of mass cultural hardware – film, telephones, radio, and microchip technology, augmented by optical fibres and digital electronics – with a common global culture. There is no global culture, only a global *market* of consumption."[15]

Some Christians see such modernity as the 'worldliness' of our day. David Wells, for example, writes: "It is, to put it bluntly, the worldliness of Our Time. For worldliness is that system of values and beliefs, behaviours and expectations, in any given culture that have at their centre the fallen human being and that relegate to their periphery any thought about God. Worldliness is that which makes sin look normal in any age and righteousness seem odd. Modernity is worldliness, and it has concealed its values so adroitly in the abundance, the comfort, and the wizardry of our age that even those who call themselves the people of God seldom recognise them for what they are."[16]

Secular Assumptions of Modernity

Undergirding modernity as a world culture and acting as its hidden infrastructure are certain secular assumptions. An assumption is an unspoken conviction, more probably imbibed through home and peers ('socialized learning') than taught explicitly, upon which you act on impulse and without thought. Assumptions form the unconscious mental map by which we live. It has been said that you can tell a person's real beliefs not by the creed he or she professes with their lips, but by the assumptions upon which they habitually act.

Modernity has developed its assumptions too, and all of us, whether we are secular in outlook or Christian, share many of those same assumptions, without realizing it. To understand modernity, we need to recognize what these are. They include:

1. *The assumption that knowledge is certain, objective and verifiable,* that we live in a rational world where anything that does not meet the criteria of reasonableness must be suspect.

Culture

"Culture...is the outward discipline in which inherited meanings and morality, beliefs and ways of behaving are preserved. It is that collectively assumed scheme of understanding that defines both what is normal and what meanings we should attach to public behaviour. It is what reveals eccentrics for their eccentricity, rebels for their rebellion, no-gooders for not doing good."[17]

What many of today's cultural critics who are raising the alarm about the drift of Western culture and its internal emptiness are saying, and what Scripture says about 'the world', are sometimes remarkably close. The difference is that secular writers see everything from a human point of view, whereas a biblical point of view always reads the world in relation to the moral character of God, and with reference to God's intentions in human history.

The one limits its perception to what is natural and discernible by the senses; the other allows the transcendent to be its filter of interpretation. The consequences of adopting either viewpoint are momentous.[18]

But Lesslie Newbigin observes: "When God created the world He did not make a spectators' gallery." That is to say, objectivity, e.g., in observation of the physical universe, is a myth. A key figure in understanding and working through this issue is Michael Polanyi and his writings.[19]

Michael Polanyi formed his experiences as a scientist visiting the Soviet Union in the 1930s. He came to the conclusion that we had been misled by the illusion of a totally objective knowledge. If all subjective elements are excluded, then it is absurd to suppose total objectivity, because if there is no subject who knows, there is no knowing.

Polanyi had the courage to confidently affirm beliefs which can be doubted, and showed that the idea of a certainty which relieves us of the need for personal commitment is an illusion, and this illusion has had a

The Superiority of Reason

An indictment of 'divinity' by the philosopher David Hume, 1711-1776: "When we run over libraries, persuaded of these principles, what havoc must we make? If we take in hand any volume; of divinity or school metaphysics, for instance; let us ask, Does it contain any abstract reasoning concerning quantity or numbers? No. Does it contain any experimental reasoning concerning matter of fact and existence? No. Commit it then to the flames: for it can contain nothing but sophistry and illusion."[20]

debilitating effect on the articulation of the Christian faith in contemporary Western society.

2. *The assumption that progress is inevitable as knowledge is acquired.* So in practice modern saviours prove to be education and science, and modern societies become suffused with a spirit of optimism.

This in turn leads to an expectation of human perfectibility, a belief that the new must always be better than the old, and that the old must invariably be inadequate and superseded. This ultimately has contributed to the spirit of consumerism in modern societies – the constant desire to have more, to have better, to measure life by what one possesses, to live for the now, to be in a process of constant change.

But how substantial and credible are these notions? Of education, Lesslie Newbigin, out of his experience as a former missionary who had lived most of his active life in India and then returned to the United Kingdom, observes: "Muslim parents in Britain are saying with increasing anger that the curriculum [they find here] as a whole is based on the assumption that the world can be understood and can be satisfactorily managed without reference to the hypothesis of God. It is not that education is neutral. There is no possible neutrality. Children...do not leave school with minds unshaped by any creed. Their minds are indeed shaped by a very definite creed, but it is not the one Christians repeat in Church."[21]

Andrew Walker describes the faith in science that is part of this creed as: "...the acceptance that science has the answers to the world's problems, based on the past performance of the prediction and control of the natural world...From the perspective of the age of steam, of the 19th century, progress seemed the stuff of the universe, and science was the key that could unlock the secrets of utopian bliss."[22]

Under modernity's creed, the consumer society has become the flag ship of this assumption of inevitable and irresistible progress. But at a cost, the price of bartering the transcendent for the transient, the ultimate for the immediate. "While the Western Dream can provide a bounty of consumer delights and technological novelties, it is incapable of providing a transcendent hope."[23]

The optimism the modernist dream engendered has been aptly described by David Lyon as a "black and white rainbow."[24] Writing of the postmodern reaction to this spirit of optimism, Philip Sampson says: "Not even a shadow [of the modernist rainbow] remains. This was a bitter disappointment to modernity, and one response to such disappointment is the postmodern incredulity towards all metanarratives. Reason is displaced by reasons, each with its own discourse and its own public. None is privileged...In modernity a particular form of rationality carried the hope of the world and collapsed beneath the weight. Postmodernity has recognised this and has rejected a false hope; but it has also rejected the possibility of reason finding its true place in the world."[25]

3. *The assumption that the autonomous self is the supreme value*, so that the individual is therefore more important than the community, and personal happiness than the corporate good. David Wells describes how the English churchman and don, Edward Norman, observed of students studying at Oxford University, their captivity to: "...the idea that life owes us personal fulfilment; that it is all about the internal development of our sensibilities and material satisfaction; that we have a wide range of 'rights' so sacred that we are justified in developing or enjoying them without regard to their effect on others; that self-expression is more important than self-control." He goes on to say that of all the shifts he has seen in the two decades 1970-1990,

especially in the world of education, he believes this will prove to be "the most far-reaching and, for man [sic], the most devastating."[26]

In many countries in the West this has been reinforced in law by legislation such as Human Rights and Privacy Acts. In New Zealand life can be marked both by daring innovative reforms, such as women's suffrage and the ordination of women to the ministry, radical steps in which much of the rest of the world follows later, but also by ghastly extravagances of 'political correctness', supposedly shaped by adherence to liberal ideals. The final decades of the 20th century in this greenhouse of social experiment yielded several examples of overzealous protection of the individual at the expense of both wider society and common sense.

A car salesman is successfully prosecuted because he advertises for a Christian staff member (the firm meets to pray before opening its doors each day). A Christian bookbinder is taken to court by an outspoken rationalist for declining to bind a set of papers denying the existence of God (even though the accused had offered to arrange an alternative bookbinder to do the work at no extra charge). A kindergarten diligently removes the pastry crosses from Easter buns so as not to offend any under-fives who may come from non-Christian homes, or who may perchance belong to another faith – while feeling no compunction about initiating the same little children in the mumbo-jumbo of Americanised Halloween with its 'tricks or treats'. Strangely, in these and other cases like them, there is no sense of the law protecting the personal position and convictions of any Christians involved.

The heavy weight of the law stands behind such idiosyncrasies of a modern society. A Human Rights Act carefully details what every individual is entitled to, but has nothing to say about the common good, and penalties to be incurred for injury to it. A Privacy Act protects individuals against information concerning them being made available to anyone else without their permission, even a quiet word by the family doctor to the mother of a 16-year-old girl who has become pregnant, or progress reports by medical staff to a husband whose wife has been committed to a psychiatric hospital for treatment.

Public Image Over Personal Character

"We have become T.S. Eliot's 'hollow men', without weight, for whom appearance and image must suffice. Image and appearance assume the functions that character and morality once had. It is now considered better to look good than to be good. The facade is more important than the substance...This accounts for the anxious search for self that is now afoot: only the hungry think about food all the time, not the well fed, and only those in whom the self is disappearing will define all of life in terms of its recovery, its actualisation."[27]

4. *The assumption that there exists an ultimate grand unified theory*, the belief that we are on the threshold of knowing everything, that truth is one and universal, unvaried and attainable, a 'theory of everything'. This leads to a proud confidence in human ability eventually to solve any problem – and for any progressive nation to assume it has all the answers for the rest at the back of the field.

5. *The assumption that reality is only that which is capable of being explained, analyzed and measured.* One way of describing what happened at the birth of the modern era is to say that there was a shift in the perception of reliable truth from a story (the story told in the Bible) to a model of reality in terms of timeless laws of nature, eternal truths of reason, of which the mathematical physics of Newton offered the supreme model.

This leads to a Newtonian, mechanistic view of the universe and to an intensely secular view of life. Followers of Newton concluded that the universe was a gigantic piece of clockwork, so everything must be clockwork.

However, John Polkinghorne, a Cambridge physicist of international standing who is also an Anglican priest, comments: "Our world does have some clocks in it, but almost all of it is clouds."[28] But because clocks are easier to understand than clouds, the temptation is to make everything a clock!

Religion is seen in the light of this to be a fancy rather than a fact, unreal to the truly modern mind and irrelevant in the truly modern world.

The assumption that all life divides into **public and private spheres.** "Each sphere tends to operate as different and unrelated realms of activity and meaning. The public sphere tends to be characterized by highly rational forms of thought, conduct and social relationship; the private sphere tends to be characterized by intimacy, particularity and emotionality."[29]

Faith, religion, and the Church in this scheme belong to the private sphere, along with all other leisure activities and, like them, constitute personal options as non-essential luxuries of life. This leads to the marginalization of the Church, contributes to the loss of status of its ministers, and encourages even the believer to separate his or her personal life before God on Sunday from his or her public life before others on Monday.

As late as 1996 some leader writers in the British quality papers were deploring any suggestions that blurred "the healthy dividing line between the spiritual and the secular". Robert Harris, for example, writing under the heading, "Three Holy Joes in a piety parade", savaged John Major, Tony Blair and Paddy Ashdown, the Conservative, Labour and Liberal party leaders respectively, for allowing personal expressions of their faith and admissions of how much their beliefs and practice of prayer entered into their everyday lives to come into the public domain.[30] Here is an example of a late modern secular assumption being given the imprimatur of a leader writer's blessing.

A decade earlier Richard John Neuhaus had devised the term 'the naked public square' to describe the consequences of thorough secularization in the public domain. In his book of the same name he wrote: "The naked public square is the result of political doctrine and practice that would exclude religion and religiously grounded values from the conduct of public business."[31]

"When religious persons are accused of trying to impose their morality upon the public policy process, it is important to ask what alternative source of morality is to be preferred, and why? If the reply is, 'it is a nonreligious morality', one should probe deeper to discover what variety of morality is being proposed."[32]

The reported remark by the founder of McDonald's applies here: "On Sunday my priorities are God, family and McDonald's – in that order; on Monday as I drive to the office I reverse the order." Os Guinness in his book *The Gravedigger File* develops an interesting thesis. As the Christian Church directly contributed to the rise of the modern world, so the modern world in its turn has undermined the Christian Church. In this sense then, and to the extent to which the Church enters, engages and employs the modern world uncritically, the Church becomes her own gravedigger.

Furthermore, as faith becomes confined to the private sphere of life, it is in danger of becoming trivialized, tailored to fit the cloth of personal preference. Robert Bellah, a sociologist, gave an account of a woman he had interviewed who expressed this spirit well: "I believe in God," she said. "I'm not a religious fanatic. I can't remember the last time I went to church. My faith has carried me a long way. It's 'Sheilaism'. Just my own little voice."[33]

The assumption that **choice** *is of the essence of life.* This promotes a pluralist view of society, where options must always be available, multiple and respected. It also contributes to the distrust of any authority beyond oneself, and of any traditional values that have not been personally chosen. In the end it creates a supermarket mentality where the customer is always king and success lies in providing constant variety and choice, while at the same time being careful not to promote one line to the disadvantage of others.

There can be three ways of employing the term 'pluralism': first, in order to acknowledge the increasing diversity of race, religion, cultures, and value systems within a given nation or community. Secondly, to describe the importance of toleration for this diversity. Most Christians would have no difficulties with these two uses of the term. Thirdly, to assert a philosophical position which insists on tolerance on the ground that all have equal validity and none can claim to be true. Some Christians (e.g., John Hick, W. Cantwell Smith, and a number involved in Religious Studies Departments of universities) would adopt this interpretation.

Cultural pluralization, which crosses national and tribal boundaries, creates a multi-layered life, no longer formed by shared histories or values, but only by common interests and needs. "We have broken up reality into

Babel and Pentecost

The story of the Tower of Babel in many ways is paralleled in the New Testament by the account of the Day of Pentecost in Acts 2. On this occasion a similar diversity of languages is described, but without the consequent confusion. In fact the exact opposite occurs. Through the power of the Gospel and the work of the Holy Spirit, the various racial and ethnic groups represented in Jerusalem that day hear the good news spoken in their own particular languages, while at the same time, in responding to the message proclaimed, they find themselves brought together in a new sense of community they hear described as "the Church". In the experience of the Church, then, it is possible to create community out of diversity. This may be an important window of opportunity for the Christian Church in addressing a postmodern world.

many little bits of digestible size", writes David Wells. But we are always having to choose between them, so a "constant barrage of changing experiences, changing scenarios, changing worlds, changing worldviews, and changing values...greatly accentuates the importance of novelty and spontaneity...We are, in fact, caught up in a whirlwind of choices that is tearing at the very foundations of our stability.

"If societies in Eastern Europe under the dominance of Marxist regimes languished from lack of choice, we languish from having too many choices to make...The relativity and impermanence of everything from values to possessions creates a deep sense of 'homelessness', even of lostness, of not belonging, of not having roots in our world."[34]

A Modern Tower of Babel

The rise of modernity has been compared by Middleton and Walsh to the building of the tower of Babel. "People's dreams and aspirations have always been embodied in cities, buildings and especially towers...Like the architects of modernity, the builders of Babel had a grand aspiration...'a tower with its

The Enlightenment Project

"Thinkers such as Descartes, Newton, and Kant provided the intellectual foundation for the modern era that was born in the late 1600s, flowered in the 1700s and 1800s, and is apparently now entering its final stage. The modern, post-Enlightenment mind assumes that knowledge is certain, objective and good. It presupposes that the rational, dispassionate self can obtain such knowledge. It presupposes that the knowing self peers at the mechanistic world as a neutral observer armed with the scientific method...believing that knowledge inevitably leads to progress and that science coupled with education will free humankind from our vulnerability to nature and all forms of social bondage...This Enlightenment quest, in turn, produced the modern technological society of the 20th century. At the heart of this society is the desire to rationally manage life, on the assumption that scientific advancement and technology provide the means to improving the quality of human life. Whatever else postmodernism may be, it embodies a rejection of the Enlightenment project, the modern technological ideal, and the philosophical assumptions upon which modernism was built."[35]

top in the heavens...let us make a name for ourselves'. For them, the sky was the limit. It is amazing how modern the Tower of Babel sounds."[36]

In the biblical account it was not the diversity of languages but their "dispersal over the face of the earth"[37] or fragmentation, and the confusion of language this brought, that was God's response to the presumptions of human achievement. Does this suggest that one of the challenges to the Christian Church in an increasing climate of postmodernity may be to address issues of a fragmented society, just as in the era of modernity it has been to address issues of human super self-confidence and an independent rationality that denies any further need of God?

Modernity is the latter-day tower of Babel. The ground floor is *science*; the second floor *technology* – in this symbolism of Western progress, the

Modern Towers of Babel

As the pyramids were to ancient Egypt, and the soaring Cathedrals to medieval Europe, so skyscrapers are to modernity. Architectural author Charles Lockwood has commented: "They are symbols of wealth, prestige and power. They are the physical manifestation of many nations' contemporary preoccupation, not with religion or monarchy but with business."

A burst of building towers took place as modernity attained its apex in the West, particularly around the Pacific rim. In part this was associated with the emergence of some Asian cities as new centres of dynamic commerce at the cutting edge of Westernization. Skyscrapers and towers became the signature skylines of Taipei, Hong Kong, Singapore and Tokyo initially, then of Jakarta, Kuala Lumpur and finally Shanghai with its new Jin Mao building, 395 metres tall and 88 storeys.

"Why has Asia become the world's leading builder of skyscrapers?" Charles Lockwood asks, in Singapore Airlines' inflight magazine in 1996. "[Because] many Asian governments and large corporations believe that highrise office buildings symbolise their power and confer prestige."[38]

Even in New Zealand, this same quest for mastery of the skyline is evident. In Auckland during the 1990s a business consortium built the 328 metre high tower of the Sky City hotel and casino complex. Insignificantly tucked in alongside this leviathan is the beautiful historic Anglican stone church of St Matthew's-in-the-City, at one time itself the signature building that stood out and gave a distinctive tone to this part of New Zealand's largest city. The Sky Tower is taller than the Eiffel Tower (320m), and its rival across the Tasman, Sydney's Centre Point (304m). Yet when it was completed, the Sky Tower ranked only seventh highest among the world's viewing and communication structures.

Ironically, the project's structural engineering director described it as an 'icon' for the City of Auckland. Or an icon of modernity, in the style of the ancient Tower of Babel!

floor which gives us power and allows us mastery over our environment. The third floor is *economic growth*. This rising building of modernity, which first had its foundations sketched out in the 15th century, took visible shape in the 17th century, was capped in the 19th century, and finally has been transformed into a mall in the 20th century, became the sign of that prosperity and progress which would in the end unite all the human race under its roof. Human progress was not only possible but inevitable – if only human autonomy be given its head. This myth has become an assumption hidden behind our school textbooks and woven into the very fabric of our common Western existence. It tells us without words that we are our own modern saviours.[38]

CHAPTER THREE

Modernity's Strengths
and Shortcomings

The Positive Face of Modernity

Whatever else may be said in criticism of the Enlightenment project and its outcome in shaping Western societies, no one can deny the many positive contributions of modernity.

One of the most significant of these has been not so much its material conquests as its commendable search for human authenticity, and the differences this has made to our dignity as persons, particularly to those without power over their own lives – the indentured Irish peasants, the African slaves, women under the domination of men, those without access to education, the underclasses. This has been described by Charles Taylor as "a powerful moral ideal at work" behind what to many critics of modernity appears at first sight to be relativism and egotism.[1] He reminds us that the other side of the coin of excessive self-centredness is liberating self-realization and self-fulfilment, not altogether to be despised, even if at times narcissistically perverted into the rampant individualism of the 'Me-generation' that emerged at the height of modernity.

Credit also needs to be given without qualification for the achievement of the modern enterprise in the many other significant benefits it has brought to humankind. A better and safer place now exists for the formerly disadvantaged in society, whose dignity and needs are today more adequately addressed and recognized. There is also the role of modernity in the steady dismantling of ancient hierarchies of power and social division.

Unfortunately however, these changes have also brought in their train new and unforeseen problems. Like the Scripture parable, sometimes a devil seven times worse than the first takes up a vacancy created by the ejection of the old. Andrew Walker observes: "...after the assassination of President Kennedy in 1963, and Martin Luther King in 1968, hero worship was increasingly relocated from political figures [one could also add, from ecclesiastical, military, missionary, visionary figures] to pop stars, fashion models, television and film actors, and sportsmen and women."[2]

That the world needs its heroes to inspire it and to bring a touch of wistful admiration into its otherwise dreary parade of mediocrity was well demonstrated in August 1997 in the worldwide wave of sorrow and grief that held the globe captive for several days following the violent and sudden death of Diana, Princess of Wales. A universal comment of appreciation was for the way she combined in one tragic figure the stuff heroes are made of: beauty, humanitarianism, courage, the common touch, and disdain by some in high office – a Joan of Arc of the 20th century.

Credit must also be paid to the modern project for its success in shedding many of the artificialities of earlier generations. People are more real today, in the sense of there being less 'airs and graces' in social relationships, more naturalness in dress and relationships. Even more significant has been the greater freedom the modern era has introduced through its espousal of the spirit of tolerance and religious liberty. Those who do hold to a religious faith today in the modernized world, despite the intense secularism of most Western societies, do so with much more sincerity, commitment and meaning. For those living within the world of late modernity, Christianity is no longer largely a social convention – it is much more a personal conviction.

Our own generation is also indebted to modernity for its creation of a healthier, longer living life on earth. Whatever arguments and debates there may be about the delivery of health services, on the average we all live longer and better. And the societies we live in comprise a wider, more accessible, more entertaining world. For a much higher proportion of people than ever before, life has the capacity for being fuller and richer than our forebears would have known in any earlier generation. We can travel further, meet more people, have access to greater amounts of information, and enjoy an unprecedented multiplicity of options and life choices. Most of us are closer to the power-brokers of our societies, have the opportunity ourselves if we wish of sharing in local or national government, and can have some influence on the course of our nations.

These tremendous gains cannot be overlooked or denied. Who today would really prefer to be living in Europe of the Middle Ages, or in the squalid urban areas of Dickensian London, or even in the gentle, unsewered Lake District of Wordsworth's England?

Modernity Expressed as Social Organisation

It would be a mistake to think of modernity simply or even principally as an intellectual movement in the realm of ideas. Particularly in its beginnings, the thoughts and writings of thinkers and philosophers opened windows to a new way of understanding and seeing our world, and to the place of humanity within it. But without another, more powerful patronage, modernity may never have attained the place it has come to occupy in the West, and in those other areas of the world that are increasingly being influenced by the West.

Modernity also needs to be understood, then, as a social order. James D. Hunter, an American social scientist writing from the Reformed tradition, states: "The reason why modernity is so distinctive and powerful is that it is a dialectic between moral understanding (e.g., the value of reason, the supreme importance of individuality, the value of tolerance and relativism), and social/institutional life. In practical terms, this means that the key ideas, values and characteristics of modernity...are 'carried' by specific institutions in three major spheres of human activity: the economy, the political and the cultural."[3]

These three carriers of modernity, Hunter tells us, are *industrial capitalism,*

Capitalism Critiqued

"Modern capitalism, or the technology and rationality that defines it, is not culturally neutral. Capitalism is probably the principal carrier of an ideology of rational control. It is here that modern individuals are socialized into a problem-solving approach to all of life and the quest for the most efficient means possible to accomplish one's objectives. The hard-nosed materialism of this reality fosters what is, in effect, a practical atheism toward everyday life."[4]

the modern state (in its bureaucratic organisation of the central areas of a nation's life), and *the knowledge sector* (including the universities, the media, the arts, and popular culture). So: "the ideas and values of the modern age are not only intellectualised, but they are embedded in powerful institutions ...something over which communities have little control and individuals even less."

Critical Thinkers and Social Organization

The way Enlightenment ideas moved from the salons of Britain and Europe into the practical organization of human life and activities was observed and encouraged by a succession of sociologists and observers.

René Descartes (1596-1650), the French philosopher, laid the foundation with his postulation of a concept of dualism, a development of his setting of the thinking self over against the objective world. This led others to divide life into the material universe which exists in its own right and cannot be influenced or interfered with by God, and the mental or spiritual world where God properly belongs. One was seen to be a public world, where factual truth was to be found; the other a private world where opinions and personal beliefs were to be confined. This is known as 'Cartesianism'.

Emile Durkheim (1858-1917), was one of the early sociologists of modernity. He interpreted the Cartesian concept as that which led to the division of labour ("differentiation" he called it) in the emerging industrial society of the 18th century. By differentiation he meant the way in which work became specialized so that one person would be skilled in one task of a process of production, another in a different task. Formerly, in old style 'cottage industries' for example, the entire process of manufacture from the sheep's back to the woven yarn sold in the local market would be performed by one person or family.

But Durkheim, and other sociologists who followed him, also saw this change as affecting the way the whole of life was increasingly coming to be viewed as belonging in different spheres. "'Work' is split off not only from 'home' but also from 'leisure', 'religion' and so on. 'Public' life was, by the same token, distinguished from 'private' in novel ways...Extended families contracted into nuclear, and became primary units of consumption rather than production. Tasks once performed by the family or the Church were taken over on the one hand by the schools, youth cultures and the mass media, or by local hospitals and welfare departments on the other."[5]

Max Weber (1864-1920) was another sociologist adding to our under-standing of how the emergence of modernity increasingly became associated with social organization following the industrial revolution, rather than remaining confined to the realm of ideas. His contribution was the recog-nition of what can be termed 'technical rationalization' (he called it "instrum-ental reason"), as a factor arising out of industrialization that introduces a more calculating attitude into life. That is, the 'rationality' of the Enlighten-ment outlook, originally a discipline of intellectual debate and enquiry, was applied as a way to reorder and control social institutions and hence society. (This is sometimes also referred to as 'functional rationality'.)

Instrumental rationality can also be described as a way of thinking that places *means/ends*, or *cause/effect* explanations where formerly *purpose* had provided meaning. So all can be discovered and understood through obser-vation, without recourse to revelation.

Predictability and efficiency are the hallmarks of instrumental rationality, whether applied to the solving of great human dilemmas, the ordering of social relationships, planning one's own life and career, or running a large production plant. Rationality does not of necessity have anything to do with

Instrumental Reason

Andrew Walker defines this concept as an echo of "the medieval under-standing of *ratio*, which suggests a notion of calculation, technique, orderliness." This in turn produces a system of rational controls which "have been institutionalized in two ways. First, through the structural institution of technological production – capitalist or communist – and the development of bureaucratic organisations. Bureaucracy is based on rational, legal procedures...dispersed throughout society by a commitment to the values of utility and rational order...through government and its agencies, schools, the workplace, and eventually the Churches themselves."

In essence, this means a world dominated by the clock, estimated for its cash value, and calculated for its utilitarian benefits. Andrew Walker comments: "What functional rationality achieves, therefore, is more insidious and pervasive than philosophical atheism: it squeezes God out not by argument but by busyness. Modern men and women are not atheists at heart: they just don't have time for religion."[6]

transcendent concepts of the common good, and is not under obligation to the past.

Weber also described this functional rationality as an 'iron cage' that has descended upon industrialized societies. This iron cage consists of a cool, rational, 'costs and benefits' approach to all human matters. The effect of this has been to diminish the realm of the spirit until it is squeezed out altogether. It can also be described as 'bureaucratic rationality', a way of ordering human existence more efficiently – but without the benefit of religion.

This bureaucratic 'iron cage' of modern societies in effect and in the end replaces the 'sacred canopy' of premodern societies. Public health provision reforms in New Zealand during the late 1980s and into the 1990s yielded very clear evidence of this. And on the broader canvas this helps explain the

A Flat and Dreary World

In a memorable passage, Max Weber more than a generation ago wrote: "With the progress of science and technology, man has stopped believing in magic powers, in spirits and demons; he has lost his sense of prophecy and, above all, his sense of the sacred. Reality has become dreary, flat and utilitarian, leaving a great void in the souls of men which they seek to fill by furious activity and through various devices and substitutes."[7]

relentless march of secularization under modernity – not a consequence essentially of intellectual arguments but of social organization.

Peter Berger, a contemporary sociologist who is also a Christian, writes of the 'modernization' of societies, meaning the social and political processes accompanying technology-led economic growth. He sees this as constituting what he terms a 'gigantic steel hammer' that smashes traditional communities, both secular and religious. In a memorable turn of phrase, Peter Berger also speaks of this producing "homeless minds", and a "world without windows."

Max Weber many years earlier had written pessimistically of the "disenchantment of the world", as older ways of life are threatened by science and technology. He saw science and technology taking 'enchantment' out of the world because they yielded no meaning, they did not show people how to live. Once 'sublime values' are extracted from public life, we are on our own. Science encourages the proliferation of disciplines, leading to a fragmentation of knowledge. There then remains no unifying vision, no ultimates by which to evaluate life, "each simply follows the demon which holds the fibres of his very life." In an earlier age, philosophy as a university discipline used to serve this unifying purpose. Now it seems only to be concerned with the process of knowing and the nature of knowledge itself. On some academic campuses it does not seem able to see the wood for the trees, and some universities have dropped it altogether! In Weber's view, life degenerates into a competition between individual values within a plural society. Science releases us from ignorance and impotence only to imprison us afresh in a world devoid of any real meaning, i.e., his 'iron cage'.

Sociologists were not the only observers to comment on the worst sides of modernity in its emergence. *John Keats* (1795-1821), one of the Romantic poets, wrote:

> Philosophy will clip an angel's wings,
> Conquer all mysteries by rule and line,
> Empty the haunted air, the gноméd mine,
> Unweave a rainbow.

In its effects on religion and religious beliefs, modernization is described as 'secularizing'. This refers to the way in which modernity by its nature moves religious faith to the margins of life, whether deliberately as an act of public policy, or incidentally as a result of the assumptions and climate of understanding it induces. In a secular society, God and those institutions which stand for God, whatever religion they represent, can have no position of advantage or prominence in the public arena. Such concerns are considered to belong to the private and personal realm. Provided that religious expressions remain in the private realm, 'off-stage', they are at least tolerated and at best respected and protected. But they have no place in the public square.[8]

"In their pride they care nothing for God:
they say in their heart that there is no God."

Psalm 10: 4, *A New Zealand Prayer Book*

Michael Polanyi (1891-1976), a neglected science philosopher who has come to be appreciated more and more for the insights he brought to the processes of change taking place, speaks of prior insights (which he describes as "tacit knowledge") of the scientist that are at first only 'strong intuition'. A scientist has a growing hunch that there is another way of interpreting the evidence, another way of explaining things. The next task is to test this out, to verify whether indeed this is the case or not – and then put it into words for others to understand.

This tacit knowledge precedes verified understanding. Polanyi says: "We always know far more than we can express." (So, for example, knowledge of the transcendent is a tacit awareness by many different peoples – and a legitimate form of knowledge – even if inexplicable.)

Is this then in some measure true of the hunch, detectable in many quite different and unconnected disciplines, that we are on the threshold of a new paradigm so far as understanding our world and our place in it is concerned? This is conveyed in a perception which artists try to express in their paintings, lyricists in their songs, writers in their novels, architects in their buildings, media editors in their presentations, etc. The academics may argue among themselves as to whether the Western world is experiencing a period of late modernity, high modernity, radicalized modernity, or post-modernity, but there are many others who just know within themselves that the thought-map of the world is changing – dramatically.

So modernity, spawned by the Age of Reason and borne by the carriers of political, economic and cultural institutions, has affected the totality of Western living to a degree never countenanced or anticipated by the fathers of the Enlightenment. Modernity, in its all-pervasive, silent way, has imposed its mark on everything Western, 'from Auschwitz to McDonald's,'[9] applying to every aspect of life the over-riding values of efficiency, calculability, predictability, and control.

Zygmunt Bauman offers a close study of the relationship of modernity to the holocaust.[10] He makes a strong case for a clear link between the technical efficiency (with absence of ethical compassion) of the Nazi concentration camps and some of the basic characteristics of the modern era. Technology always runs this risk when removed from a close relationship with a spiritual and moral base.

Neil Postman writes: "Adolf Eichmann becomes the basic model and metaphor for a bureaucrat in the age of Technopoly. When faced with the charge of crimes against humanity, he argued that he had no part in the formulation of Nazi political or sociological theory; he dealt only with the technical problems of moving vast numbers of people from one place to another. Why they were being moved and, especially, what would happen to them when they arrived at their destination were not relevant to his job."[11]

The Downside of Modernity

Modernity, then, also has its downside. The principle negative effects of modernity on contemporary life in Western societies need to be identified, as some of these have imperceptibly contributed to the response now being recognised as postmodernity.

In the first place, modernity has led to an unprecedented *elevation of the individual and of personal rights* – at considerable cost to community and social responsibility, and to family life. Not only Christians are evincing deep concern over the drift to 'rampant individualism' in Western societies under the impact of modernity. In Britain a leading member of the Jewish Community, Lord Jacobovits, late in 1996 wrote in a leading British weekly: "Our contemporaries speak and think in terms of rights – of what others owe us, of what we can demand. Our [Jewish] tradition speaks only of duties and obligations we owe to others. Our basic imperatives are The Ten Commandments, not a Bill of Rights."[12]

Robert N. Bellah has written of the way this particular aspect of modernity has infected the Christian Church, adding to the difficulties not only of pro-claiming the Gospel of Christ in such a climate, but also of retaining the loyalty and commitment of its members. He writes: "Christian leadership is faced with the difficulty of communicating the deep social realism of biblical religion to an individualistic culture. This individualistic heritage, so suscep-tible to defining the human as relentless market maximizer, has reduced the notion of common good to that of the sum of individual goods. 'Consumer Christians' may see the Church as simply existing to 'meet their needs', but having no claim to their commitment and loyalty...But in the complex inter-dependent world in which we live, the sum of our individual goods produces a common bad, that eventually erodes our individual satisfactions as well."[13]

This emphasis on the role of the individual has had a long and powerful impact on the development of Western economies, extending over several centuries. But it is only in this century that 'private enterprise' has led to the emergence of the market as the driving force of many modern societies. While proving profitable for the competent and the capable, and achieving remarkable transformation of some economies, the doctrinaire acceptance of 'market forces' as the determinant factor in shaping society has often been disastrous for those who do not possess the same ability or opportunity to work the system.

Some observers see this inflation of the individual and personal rights as leading to a moral relativism that has had ill-effects on family life and the framework of security many children need as they acquire the skills and experience that will equip them for adulthood. In 1996 Melanie Phillips published a book in the United Kingdom, *All Must Have Prizes*, that was a critique of what she perceived as the current moral relativism. She was ferociously attacked in the British press by what she describes as "the education establishment and other cultural custodians."[14]

"Britain is in the grips of a culture war" she wrote. "In one camp are the libertarian individualists, who won't distinguish between good and bad behaviour because they think the equality of free choices is sacrosanct. In the other are those who think judgment between right and wrong and an assertion of the common good are essential for a civilized social ethic." Melanie Phillips explains that her book "argues that moral norms have frayed because of a breakdown in the role of education in nurturing the young."

The moral hierarchy which sets adults in authority over children has been eroded. The idea that there is *any* superior wisdom or authority to be transmitted has been undermined, with catastrophic effects in the classroom no less than in family life. Destructive processes are also at work in the family, where rules, structures and boundaries are dissolving in the face of the relentless march of adults' and children's 'rights'. As children are given adult responsibilities, adults are infantilized. The permanent commitment and care inherent in parental duty have become conditional upon adult 'rights' to sexual gratification and personal fulfilment, which have contributed to the fracture of the two-parent family. Parental authority has been undermined by the inappropriate doctrine of children's autonomy, which has made punishment taboo and discipline a dirty word.

"So at home and at school, the narrative which anchors children in time and place, and against which they can securely define themselves, has fragmented. Is it surprising, then, that more and more children seek attention through outrageous or criminal behaviour, and suffer increasing rates of depression, eating disorders, educational under-achievement and other signs of confusion and distress?"

Personal Freedom

Associated with this emphasis on the individual and on his or her rights under modernity there has also been a relentless pursuit of *greater personal freedom*. But this has been at a frightening cost – the price of greater individual and social alienation and anomie.[15]

Peter Berger calls this "the nightmare par excellence, where the individual is submerged in a world of disorder, senselessness and madness."[16] In cities, though always surrounded by people and entertainment centres and throbbing urban life, there is often also terrible loneliness and lostness, more so than in rural areas.

In the modern world there is much fear, but there is even more anxiety – in the sense of powerlessness, an inability to control the circumstances of personal life, a feeling of being pawns in a game played by irresistible and unpredictable forces in society (Kierkegaard called it "dread"). The effect is to greatly destabilize the self and seriously undermine one's capacity to cope in life. "Stripped of external connectedness and haunted within by anxiety, modern individuals drift in society. Filled with dread, dis-ease and foreboding and unable to secure a foothold in any external reality, they take refuge in the one certain reality remaining – the self...The mass media now churn out such a multitude of images, desirable personae, styles to be adopted and emulated that the young...are left choking in confusion and sometimes despair. They have no internal gyroscope to help them settle on a direction amid the countless competing 'products' in the market."[17]

Untrammelled personal freedom also brings new insecurities as old and familiar community boundaries and cultural landmarks are removed. An editorial in a leading paper at the height of the debate in Great Britain over the teaching of moral values observed: "Today, they say, we are all mere individuals swept up in a worldwide movement of money and markets which make a single community, even a nation, increasingly unable to set its own rules." The article later spoke about the impossibility many felt of doing anything about it in face of "a sense of powerlessness against the international forces of modernity."[19]

The aged and adolescent youth are particularly vulnerable at such a time. Does this help explain the seemingly unrelated significance of, on the one hand, the rise in 'grey power' and, on the other hand, the increasing incidence of youth suicides in New Zealand, together with the mounting youth violence in Great Britain, over the last two decades of the 20th century? Freedom has never come cheaply.

Violence in British Schools

In October 1996 both the British public and the politicians in Westminster were generally of one mind that there was a culture of violence in the nation which reached right down into the schools. The Dunblane disaster (although it involved an adult as the perpetrator) had already alerted the nation to a mindless streak of violence in their midst. Then followed the senseless murder of Headmaster Philip Lawrence outside his school gates by a knife wielding, disgruntled 16-year-old schoolboy. Not long after this an entire West Ridings (UK) school staff threatened to resign unless 60 unmanageable children were expelled from the school. In a short space of time these and similar incidents provoked a swelling wave of concern over what was happening to British society. The consensus was that a generation was emerging who had little sense of moral responsibility or civic virtues. Some blamed the thrust of education policies over previous decades which had elevated the individual and his or her personal rights above community responsibilities and duties.

Over the following days responses to this call for action flowed in from all quarters. Some advocated greater powers of exclusion (suspension) of recalcitrant pupils for head teachers and governing bodies; others pushed for compulsory classes in civics and good citizenship, with changes to the curricula to enable this. One proposal was to require contracts between parents and school before admission of a pupil. There was a strong move from Conservative Government backbenchers to require a smarter dress code for teachers, and from front benchers in the House of Commons to legislate for the reintroduction of caning and corporal punishment in the schools.

What was missing from the plethora of proposals was any suggestion that the problem was at root a spiritual one, in that the steady secularization of society had gradually been removing any strong sense of individual or corporate accountability to God for one's personal or public conduct. Some form of tinkering with the existing system was universally seen as the way forward. God, however, was given no place in this projected renewal of British character and public morality.

As the United Kingdom debated issues of a national morality and the need for new directions in the face of rising problems among the young, Nicholas Tate writing in *The Times* described "four modern fallacies about morality we need to tackle if we are to support schools and parents in promoting the moral development of young people.

"The first is the fallacy that because we are now such a pluralistic society ...we do not and cannot, *ipso facto*, share a common moral code." Nicholas Tate challenged this assumption, and took issue with the response of "some members of our weary metropolitan intelligentsia...Their attitudes – contemptuous of tradition, excited by the novel and bizarre, dismissive of the concerns of ordinary people – have been at the root of our moral confusion...

"The second fallacy is that moral opinions are no different from tastes and preferences, that there is no more point in arguing about moral matters than about tastes in food or foreign holidays. This kind of moral relativism is linked to the idea that our society is now so pluralistic that all we can do is agree to disagree...The third fallacy is that the supreme value is respect and tolerance...a reflection of what, outside schools, has sometimes come to seem like a 'no blame, no shame' society....

"Finally there is the fallacy that, because it is legal to do something, it must be acceptable to do it. We have become reluctant to condemn people exercising their legal rights." Tate questioned the validity of this reasoning which, he claimed, failed to recognise the possibility of wrongdoing *within* the law.

He concluded his argument by inviting society to recognise these fallacies, which "means putting responsibilities before rights. It means reviving our sense that we belong to a civic society with a shared moral code and a common culture. It means recognising that there is a moral dimension to every aspect of our lives."[19]

Narcissism

Modernity also brought with it a narcissistic *preoccupation with 'the self'*, an obsession that goes far beyond any search for authenticity. "Descartes, who sat alone gazing at his fire and scouring his mind for indubitable truth, is doomed to recognize as his proper heir the solitary soul couched in front of a television set, seeking satisfaction for unspecified needs and ineffable desires."[20] Advertising plays on this obsession. "You deserve it", the promotions shout. Glossy magazines survive on it, whether the 'self' is the reader or some cult hero elevated by the media in order to endorse articles on self-improvement, courses on self-fulfilment, and appeals to self-potential. Even education systems build curricula upon it, accepting as their goal: "Each child will be encouraged to discover and develop their full potential" – without any recognition of the dark side of the potential in all humanity. And always hovering, awaiting a wrong move or an inappropriate word, are the Civil Libertarians and the Political Correctness watchers to protect this obsession's more bizarre expressions and anti-social representations.

Modernity has redefined the 'self' as the 'autonomous self' by reducing the influence of any transcendent reference point, removing the credibility of any overarching explanation of life, and thus driving the self in upon itself for meaning and value. Yet the self has proved altogether inadequate to bear this burden, and this has led to a distortion of feelings and intuitions in order to fill this void. "The fragile self adrift in the relentless tumult of modernity inevitably begins to experience the emptiness and weariness to

TV Dinners and Moral Decline

"There seems to be a consensus", writes columnist Matthew Fort, "that we are in the middle of a moral and social crisis – delinquent children, irresponsible parents, rising crime, schools that make our prisons look like models of good order, tacitly accepted bribery of politicians, business incompetence being richly rewarded, the lack of personal responsibility among politicians, commercial leaders and so on.

"There seems to be a growing belief that these ills may in part at any rate, be blamed on the decline of the family as a social unit. Parents ...no longer accept responsibility for disciplining their children, and children no longer look to the family as the source of their moral or social values. In other words, there is no transfer of the experience and values of one generation to the next...

"So how did previous generations grow up with a sense of right and wrong, and responsibilities to a community? The answer lies in that pre-TV dinner age when families sat down together to eat...the kitchen table was the debating chamber...

"It is worth considering some statistics. Since 1971, two years after we [in Great Britain] began to find the lure of TV dinners irresistible, the rate of divorce has increased sixfold, the number of single families has tripled, and more than 25 percent of households consist of a single parent living alone...

"The symbolism of the Last Supper and the act of communion is lost on our supposedly God-fearing politicians...We eat in haste, but we repent at our leisure."[21]

which postmodern writers, artists and composers have so uniformly pointed. This agonising sense of weightlessness that we once thought only God would suffer in modern culture now turns out to be ours as well. This development has brought Western culture, both high and low, to the point of obsession with the autonomy of the self and to a corresponding rejection of all other authorities."

The common assumption behind the self movement is the perfectibility of human nature. The biblical Gospel asserts the very reverse – that the self is flawed, and maladjusted in its relationship to both God and others. David Wells writes: "Where the self describes the locus of the faith, good and evil are reduced to a sense of well-being or its absence. Theology then becomes therapy, the desire for righteousness is replaced by a search for happiness, holiness by wholeness, truth by feeling, ethics by feeling good about one's self."[22]

Reinhold Niebuhr observed that the self draws its substance from three basic sources: family, community, and craft. Connections to each of these are now either strained or lost to the modern self.

- *The family* – through widespread divorce, single-parent households, marriage strains. See: *TV Dinners*.
- A sense of *community* – diminished through constant mobility and rootlessness.
- *Craft* – loses out to machines, concealed by layers of bureaucracy, and career changes.

Pluralism

A further aspect of the downside of modernity has been its development of a public policy of *respect for difference (pluralism)*. Students of the world's other religions have learned to respect and honour the many helpful insights of those religions, but some Christians have done so at the expense of minimizing their own faith claims and distinctives.

For some, this has been a reaction against a perceived arrogance, colonialism, and presumed superiority that they felt sometimes coloured Christian missions. "The result has been a 'democratization' of religious claims that can lead to a denigration of some of the fundamental beliefs of their own faith. In doing so they have fallen backwards into another kind of arrogance, obscuring the magnificent truths implicit and explicit in Christ's crucified love. Therefore one of the greatest global challenges will be to discover how we can have healthy and open ended dialogue with other faiths without compromising the uniqueness of the claims of Christ."[23]

The most productive dialogue takes place between people committed to the confident truth of their own religious traditions, yet open to listen and learn from others. Otherwise this will be at the expense of some loss of social cohesiveness, particularly a sense of being a community where all publicly, if not personally, and in common possess a shared faith and confess a divine story that provide the social cement binding that community together.

This respect for difference also has had the effect of encouraging a resurgent tribalism of the late 20th century. In time this may prove to be much more significant than the rise of nation states in the late 19th century. Gene Veith notes "...the emergence of a new tribalism...The combination of social changes, technological developments, and postmodernist ideology has undermined the very principle of a unified national culture and has driven individuals to find their identities in subcultures." Veith identifies the breakdown of the family and social mobility as two of the other principal contributory factors.

He goes on to observe that whereas under the influence of modernity respect for difference was counter-balanced by forces emphasising the essential unity of society, under the influence of *post*modernity respect for difference becomes stress on the *dis*unity of society, "embracing separatism in the name of diversity". Veith continues: "Today from Africa to India, from Serbian nationalism to the neo-tribal structures of American street gangs, once unified societies are fracturing into tribes at war with each other. Going beyond the modern, being postmodern, sometimes is nothing more than the rebirth of the primitive."[24]

There are, it cannot be denied, 'meeting points' that draw people together apart from race and place, but they do not create community. For example, Chris Rojek writes about "the symbolic gathering around brandnames such as Nike, Apple Macintosh, Nintendo, Calvin Klein and so on, where consumers recognize their tribal status but retain an essentially nomadic existence."[25]

Loss of a Sense of the Sacred

In introducing a more positive concern for the temporal, modernity has also brought about a corresponding *loss of a sense of the sacred*. This trend became very noticeable in various parts of the Western world from the early 1980s. As early as 1979, the observation was being made that "...from the religious point of view, humanity has entered a long night that will become darker and darker with the passing of the generations and of which no end can yet be seen. It is a night in which there seems to be no place for a conception of God, or for a sense of the sacred, and ancient ways of giving significance to our own existence, of confirming life and death, are becoming increasingly untenable."[26]

This can be discerned in New Zealand as well as in many other countries in the increased level of vandalism involving church buildings, and in the inroads made by sporting events and retail trading into the traditional 'sabbath' regard for the Sunday of Christendom. Sacred spaces as well as sacred places no longer have significant public respect.

Even an arch enemy of organized religion, Karl Marx, could see this coming. In *The Communist Manifesto* Marx expressed it in these terms: "Constant revolutionizing of production, uninterrupted disturbance of all social relations, everlasting uncertainty and agitation, distinguish the bourgeois epoch from all earlier ones...All that is solid melts into air, all that is holy is profaned..."

But there is also a further dimension to this loss of respect for the transcendent in a marked decline among professional classes of a sense of personal accountability, as modernity has reached its apogee. Integrity either in public business or in private morality cannot at the end of the 20th century be assumed as an integral part of professional life.

This is true even within the administration of the Church. In the UK, *The Times*[27] reported misappropriation of almost £240,000 by a diocesan accountant, working for the Church of England under his clerical father-in-law. The report observed: "For centuries the diocese conducted its financial affairs on the basis that people claiming to be Christians were worthy of trust. Gentleman's agreements and familial relationships set up bonds of loyalty that did as much as the law and any number of accountants to secure parish funds for posterity. But with the rise of materialism and secularism in the 1980s and 1990s, it became clear that traditional and sometimes eccentric ways of running church finances were not enough."

Modernity and Education Philosophy

John Dewey (1859-1952) has probably been the most representative intellectual proponent in recent times of the spirit of modernity. His philosophy of education permeated the state school system in many parts of the Western world. He described the spirit of modern life in terms of four changes from the premodern period in Western history.[28]

- *Modernity is no longer preoccupied with the supernatural*, but rather delights in the natural, the this-worldly, and the secular.
- Instead of the medieval emphasis on submission to ecclesiastical authority, "there is a *growing belief in the power of individual minds*, guided by methods of observation, experience and reflection, to attain the truths needed for the guidance of life."
- *Belief in progress.* "Man is capable, if he will but exercise the required courage, intelligence and effort, of shaping his own fate."
- '*The patient and experimental study of nature*, bearing fruit in inventions which control nature and subdue her forces to social use, is the method by which progress is made.'

Dewey's modern man stands out as self-assured, autonomous, liberated, and rational. But is this a realistic assessment? Will the untutored soul, relieved of the constrictions of the past, find maturity of character and conduct simply by being free? Need virtue be taught, sanctions established for the recalcitrant? There are those who see the human lot differently and who argue for a more pro-active policy of education. An English newspaper editorial, for example, under the headline 'Virtue Must Be Taught – Why moral neutrality is immoral and self-defeating', argued: "If communal duties are to be restored alongside communal rights, a range of sanctions must be ready for those whose only idea of one's duty is not doing it...As for reducing freedoms, a successful lesson in the difference between right and wrong prevents no one from doing wrong if he or she so chooses; but surely it is better if individuals know what is wrong and are aware of society's sanctions."

"Studied neutrality and moral relativism are, in themselves, immoral. Refusing to warn the vulnerable that they will suffer if they yield to untutored impulses is an abdication of responsibility...The result of teaching no virtues at all is a desiccated discourse whose dry emptiness extends far beyond the civics class. And into the vacuum left by the fear of teaching virtue imperfectly march the intolerance, incomprehension and fascination with extremists that the liberal minded citizen rightly condemns."[29]

Evaluating Modernity

Alongside all the many good things that may be said in its defence, modernity has also undeniably accelerated urbanization, increased social mobility, and contributed to neighbourhood anonymity. Gene Veith observes: "Modernism, in its social applications, homogenized society. Unity was achieved by obliterating past traditions in the name of progress. Technological standardization eroded the sense of place and the sense of local identity...As a result of modernization, the commercial strips in just about every small town, suburb, and big city look pretty much the same."[30] Like a carrot held out in front of a donkey, modernity created a climate of expectation that there would be inexorable, unbroken evolutionary progress toward the end goals of human perfectibility and one unified world of peace and harmony.

Taking the fair measure of modernity involves weighing the positives against the negatives. "William James said the debate about modernity is between the tough and the tender. For the tough, the destruction of old traditions creates new freedoms, new knowledge, new opportunities. For the tender, the price of all this destruction is simply too high: progress is purchased at the price of justice, belonging and community."[31]

This evaluation will also involve assessing more closely the varying roles and relationships of philosophers, artists and captains of industry, i.e., epistemological, cultural and institutional factors, both in generating and in developing modernity, whether their role is as creators or conveyors of modernity. There is considerable debate over which is the cart and which is

Social Consequences

"All of this and much more has for millions of people created a gap between vision and reality that, in turn, has precipitated a crisis in their worldview and self-understanding. This has not happened at the level of the individual alone but also in respect of entire communities. And when such a crisis involves the dominant visions of a particular society, as is the case today, the entire society is prone to massive breakdown. The very scaffolding on which people are standing is collapsing."

David Bosch

the horse, and indeed who is the driver in charge of the vehicle of modernity. Walter Brueggemann, for example, sees modernity as the "large intellectual environment of the Enlightenment."[32]

The consensus emerging seems to be that *rationality* (as a way of interpreting the world we live in) has been in the driving seat of modernity. This in turn would have got nowhere without the vehicle of *social organization* (as the carrier of modernity). But social organization has itself been led by the animal energy of both *high and pop culture* (understood in the widest sense as the imaginative, freewheeling creativity of all who strain against the constricting harness of contemporary life and values – i.e., advertising agencies as well as artists, paparazzi as well as poets.) This is an interim assessment. Our generation still stands too close to the summit of the modern era to be in a position to assess confidently its ultimate contribution to the good of humanity or to the fulfilment of the purposes of God.

Questions That Remain

Were those who contributed by whatever way to the emergence of modernity simply acting upon the dynamics of a paradigm change that was bound to happen anyway – or were they making it happen? Similarly, is the new mood of *post*modernity today infiltrating Western societies by design, or merely to fill a growing vacuum? Or can postmodernity rather be explained as an unconscious counter-reaction to the perceived negative impact of modernity?

Is anyone in the driver's seat, or is the downhill momentum of modernity just drawing postmodernity after it, with gathering speed? Is art an intuitive reflection of this, a prophetic anticipation of where things are heading? Do the philosophers and thinkers of the Western world simply provide an explanation of what is happening, a sort of Guide Friday commentary on the way as we take our place up on the open deck, telling us what to look out for and the significance of things we might otherwise have passed by and overlooked? Or are they trailblazers, beckoning writers, editors, teachers and planners to follow them? Zygmunt Bauman maintains that "intellectuals no longer legislate, they just interpret."[33]

Who leads? Or in the end is a paradigm shift, as a fundamental change in the essential nature of society, the outcome of a myriad of unplanned and loosely related human responses to where the world has brought them? Are particular philosophers, artists and leaders merely the keyholders who open the gates, the secular prophets who anticipate and interpret the mood, the midwives who attend the birth and assist in the labour?

And where is God in all this? Where should the Church be found – waiting to one side in the dressing room in case it is called upon, or already on centre stage ready to play its part on cue? Nicholas Wolterstorff has a clear mind in this matter. He writes: "Christianity is ineffective in shaping our public life. What effectively shapes our public life and our society generally is our adulation of science and technology and economic growth. Christianity for the most part stands in the wings and watches."[34]

CHAPTER FOUR

The Emergence
of Postmodernity

As modernity began to reach the pinnacle of its achievements in the 1960s and 1970s, signs of a reaction against its precepts and programmes were also becoming increasingly evident. This late 20th century response to modernity is now generally being spoken of as 'postmodernity'. Social scientist Anthony Giddens argues the case for seeing postmodernity as "modernity coming to understand itself" rather than as the overcoming of modernity itself.[1] Like other culture shifts, postmodernity had been incubating for some time, its presence gradually beginning to be felt only in some sectors of Western culture.

But around 1970 a wider public became aware of this new spirit of postmodernity, and increasingly began to write about it. In the *Social Science Citations Index*, for example, the number of entries for the word 'postmodern' and related terms over the five year period leading up to 1991 rose from 17 to 276.[2] Sociologist David Harvey writes: "Somewhere between 1968 and 1972...we see postmodernism emerge as full-blown though still incoherent movement out of the chrysalis of the anti-modern movement of the 1960s... With respect to architecture, for example, Charles Jencks dates the symbolic end of modernism and the passage to the postmodern as...15 July 1972, when the Pruitt-Igoe housing development in St Louis (a prize-winning version of Corbusier's 'machine for modern living') was dynamited as an uninhabitable environment for the low-income people it housed."[3]

But others see the development of postmodernism stretching over half a century. Stanley Grenz for example describes this as a process that began as far back as 1930. As he reads the birth of postmodernity, the labour stages were these:

1930s...witnessed the first inklings of postmodernity (i.e., even before modernity had reached the dizzy heights of its own self-confidence and expression.)

1960s...postmodernism first appeared on the fringes of society, becoming attractive to architects, artists and thinkers.

1970s...the postmodern challenge to modernity infiltrated further into mainstream culture, eventually in the course of this decade as the overarching label for a diverse social and cultural phenomenon. Hans Bertens comments: "Up to the early 1980s the debate on postmodernism remained almost exclusively confined to architecture and to the arts, even if some of the critics involved were more than willing to diagnose a new Zeitgeist [spirit of the times]. But all of that would change dramatically in the course of the 1980s when postmodernism began to engage the serious attention of professional philosophers and of leftist critics."[4]

1980s...this mood became more pronounced, perceptible, and public, invading pop culture and the market place of mainstream society. "Postmodernism assumes various forms", writes Grenz. "It is embodied in certain attitudes and expressions that touch the day-to-day lives of a broad diversity of people in contemporary society. Such expressions range from fashions to television and include such pervasive aspects of popular culture as music and film. Postmodernism is likewise incarnated in a variety of cultural expressions, including architecture, art and literature. But postmodernism is above all an intellectual outlook."[5]

The response of postmodernity paralleled the changes that were taking place as an industrial society gave way to an information society following the application in 1971 of the microchip to communications technology. In this sense it can be seen as an outcome of concurrent social changes. But once again its primitive origins were in the realm of ideas and can be traced back to the thinking and writings of Friedrich Nietzsche.

Nietzsche

In 1883 Friedrich Nietzsche (1844-1900) published *Also Sprach Zarathustra*. This spelled the beginning of the end of modernity and inaugurated the gestation period of postmodernity. The modern era had emerged out of an intellectual revolution that challenged the assumptions of medieval philosophy and science. Modernity in turn began to unravel when a similar revolution challenged the explanatory power of 'modern' categories.

It was Nietzsche, then, who fired the first salvo against the Enlightenment establishment, and it is he, if anyone, who deserves the accolade of patron saint of postmodern philosophy. He consistently showed himself to be the foe of modernity. Basically Nietzsche rejected the Enlightenment concept of truth. He maintained that the world consists of many fragments of reality, totally different from one another. In seeking to impose upon these a generalized concept, we destroy the complexity, deny the richness, and diminish the vitality of life and human experience – i.e., we distort what is. So, Nietzsche claims, rationalistic human knowledge is a purely human creation. In arranging the world in categories, we are disarranging reality.[6]

This makes Nietzsche in the end a nihilist. Ultimately, he claims, we have no access to reality whatsoever. There can be no "true world". Everything is merely a "perspectival appearance", the origin of which lies within ourselves. We live in a constructed world that comes from our own way of looking. The "will to power" is the ultimate determinant. That is, whoever has the strongest will and the ability to enforce it, whether by use of arms or arguments, determines what the truth of the matter is.

The Spirit of Postmodernity

Features that mark the new mood of postmodernity fall into several clusters:

First, **fragmentation**. If, during the period of modernity and until quite recently, one could still speak in any sense of a 'sacred canopy' sheltering the culture of a continent (fractured though it might be, and with innumerable holes appearing in it), with the advent of postmodernity we find that a canopy has incontrovertibly disappeared, to be replaced instead by millions of small tents.[7] Theological College principal Graham Cray expresses it in this way: "Life is also fragmented. Academic disciplines tend to develop in isolation from one another. We are a society of the expert, yet lacking a shared sense of the meaning and coherence of the whole. Our identity seems to depend on a variety of roles we are expected to play in different contexts. We are to be one person at work, another at home, another at leisure, with little sense of any personal centre or any set of integrating relationships."[8]

No longer was there to be any suggestion or pretence of assuming that there is a single, grand meaning to the universe or one ultimately true explanation for life.[9] Each person, each community, each distinct ethnic group has its own story to tell and to follow, its own worldview to convey its identity There is no need for everyone to conform, no need for unity of outlook, no external authority of religion, science, philosophy or the state that should any longer insist on its story being the superior discourse. The remedy for the ills of the world most typically prescribed by postmodern thinkers is the free play of difference. We are to renounce the desire for metanarratives which claim to know and tell the story of the world and, instead, to embrace heterogeneity, allowing for a range of local stories that reflect the character of different groups of people.

Lesslie Newbigin distinguishes between three widely held worldviews that seek to explain human relationships. One is represented by the image of the ocean, in which all human beings are submerged in a greater whole so as to lose their individual identity. This is the position adopted by some of the great world religions, e.g., Buddhism. Then there is the view that sees human beings as like pebbles on a beach, brought together because of spatial proximity, but each a totally separate and distinct object. Late modernity has promoted this view of humanity. The third image is that of the web, where space and difference is allowed but where each is inextricably linked to and dependent on the others in a network of connection. Newbigin suggests this is the Christian worldview, preserving together the distinctiveness of the individual with the interdependence of the community.

Such an understanding of individual human worth alongside the need for corporate responsibility may be an area where Christian insights and experience (where not themselves weakened by the acids of modernity) can contribute significantly as the mood of postmodernity settles over the Western world.

For Christians, an understanding of the Trinity can yield valuable insights as to how the discrete individual can at the same time be part of the integrated community. The paradox of the Trinity does not require a choice between an autonomous One and an undivided Three. Nor does it require discovering some intermediate common ground on which to stand, where both the One and the Three have to resign something of their essential character for this to happen.

The doctrine of the Trinity offers an affirmation of the uniqueness of each person of the Godhead while at the same time the indispensability of the Three-in-One. The very irrationality of such an insight, strange as it may seem, may well appeal more to the postmodern mind than it ever did to the rational mind of the modern.

Metanarratives of Modernity

This postmodern mood, then, involves the rejection of all master stories, whether spiritual, social or economic – e.g., the Marxist economic analysis of society, the Freudian account of the human psyche, the scientific rationalism that postulates endless and inevitable progress, but also the biblical account of the origin and destination of the created world. Jean-Francois Lyotard was one of the early analysts of 'the postmodern condition' (in fact, a report he wrote for the French Government was given this title). His most quoted statement was: *"Simplifying to the extreme, I define **postmodern** as incredulity toward metanarratives"* (i.e., any accounts whatsoever that claim to explain the world, its meaning and destiny).

Andrew Walker observes: "Master narratives of progress...continued sporadically throughout the 19th century. Darwin's *On the Origin of the Species*, published in 1859, spawned a host of neo-Darwinisms, from Herbert Spencer's sociology to Fabian socialism. James Frazer's anthropology in *The*

Golden Bough clearly followed in the footsteps of Strauss and Comte. And if Adam Smith's *Wealth of Nations*, first published in 1776, did not quite live up to the status of a metanarrative, capitalism itself provided the infrastructure for a mythology of progress for the liberal democracies right to the end of the 20th century."[10]

So perceptions of truth and reality have undergone a radical change. Truth is much less something that exists objectively outside of ourselves – it is whatever we believe has meaning for us, for this moment. Reality is what we create; some would go so far as to claim, what we create by our use of language. We make our own worlds. One way of describing postmodernism is 'unprincipled pragmatism', just a tad kinder than 'nihilism with a smile'!

Such a way of seeing the world reinforces the pluralism that was important even in the climate of late modernity – but with a new twist. Instead of advocacy of *respect for other points of view* alongside confidence in the truth of one's own, the pluralism of postmodernity says that there exists a *plurality of truths*, any of which can be true only for those who hold them. No one of them can ultimately be shown to be true for everyone.

Writing in the context of late modernity, and pointing out the absurdity of the selective pluralism of that time, Lesslie Newbigin observes: "We take pride in being a pluralist society...but this pluralism does not extend to the world of 'facts'. When we disagree about what are called facts, we do not see this as an occasion to celebrate our pluralism – we work hard at establishing which position is right, and readily point out error in points of view we believe to be inadequate."[11]

Furthermore, where the late modernist was a strong individualist, insisting that "we are each entitled to our own opinion", the postmodernist places more emphasis on the collective values and picture of the world held by each social group, and their interaction. The remedy for the ills of the world most typically prescribed by postmodern thinkers is the free interplay of difference. We are to renounce the desire for metanarratives which claim to know and tell the story of the world and, instead, to embrace heterogeneity, allowing for a range of local stories that reflect the character of different groups of people.[12]

Surface Significance

A second distinguishing cluster of features that mark postmodernity is an emphasis on *surface significance*. There is a style increasingly associated with the mood of postmodernity that exalts the surface at the expense of the depth. Frederic Jameson describes this as "a perpetual present, without depth, definition or secure identity."[13] This is often reflected in its art, dress styles and architecture. Gene Veith writes: "...some [civic] communities are trying to restore a sense of regional and local personality. Such attempts, in the postmodern way, often deal with the surface rather than substance. (Developers often painstakingly restore historically rich 19th century buildings on the outside and then install a shopping mall on the inside.)"[14]

'Bricolage' as a clothing style, is another example. In pointed defiance of the modern endeavour to co-ordinate individual pieces of clothing in a unified look, the postmodern may intentionally juxtapose incompatible or heterogeneous elements, such as garments and accessories, from each of the preceding four decades. The same can be said of building design. Frederic Jameson comments: "Postmodernism no longer produces monumental works ...but ceaselessly reshuffles the fragments of pre-existent texts, the building blocks of older cultural and societal productions, in some new and heightened bricolage." Sometimes this is referred to as a 'pick 'n mix' feature of postmodernity, discernible not just in fashion but also as a hallmark of the wider culture of postmodernity.

For the postmodern, it is the visual image that matters; it is being projected as a 'sign' that has more reality than what it represents, and as a tool for creating and refashioning one's own reality. This in turn introduces a sense of *playfulness* into the world of postmodernity, as a reaction against the perceived over-seriousness of late modernity, "a re-enchantment of the world that modernity tried hard to dis-enchant." Why should the postmodern feel bound to any demand or expectation outside him or herself? Life should not be static or conformist, but innovative, free-flowing, unrestrained, rejoicing in difference and always on the move.

Michel Foucault, the archetypal postmodernist writer and thinker, in 1983 urged us to "develop action, thought and desires by proliferation, juxtaposition, and disjunction [and] to prefer what is positive and multiple, difference over uniformity, flows over unities, mobile arrangements over systems. Believe that what is productive is not sedentary but nomadic."[15] Hence Foucault's ideal of a *heterotopia* rather than a *utopia* as the desired goal of postmodernism.

A postmodern writer, Jean Baudrillard, breaks down the shift from word to image into four stages through which the 'sign' has taken over from reality:

- The sign as *the reflection of a basic reality*: e.g., clothing worn reflects one's position in society.
- The sign *masks and perverts a basic reality*.
- The sign *masks the absence of a basic reality*.
- The sign *bears no relation to any reality whatsoever*.

Baudrillard sees postmodern culture as located at this fourth stage. Images are endlessly produced without any attempt to bed them in reality. He terms this 'hyper-real'. So in postmodernism, culture is dominated by simulations – signs, codes, and ambiguous images. Forget the depth, enjoy the surface. The catch phrase of the age is 'What you see is what you get.'[16]

Perpetual Present

Another cluster of features of postmodernity can be described as an experience of a **perpetual present**. Featherstone writes: "On the level of everyday cultural experiences, postmodernism implies the transformation of reality into images, and the fragmentation of time into a series of perpetual presents."[17]

History loses its significance as the past is relegated to the lumber room as a dimension of life with no more use than as a fetching repository of experiences and styles available to be ransacked at will for enriching and enlivening the present. So the style of postmodernity becomes that of eclecticism, taking whatever suits and appeals to mix it up in a timeless juxtaposition of periods and images, "the random cannibalisation of all the styles of the past."[18]

Perpetual present distorts time like a crazy mirror in sideshow alley. David Harvey writes: "I want to suggest that we have been experiencing, these last two decades, an intense phase of time-space compression that has

Peter Blake

In art in the United Kingdom, an example of this eclecticism and juxta-position of disparate objects is the work of Peter Blake. In 1996-97 the National Gallery mounted an exhibition of his work, *Now We Are 64*, in close association with several paintings by an eminent African expatriate, Cheeta! (Cheeta is a chimpanzee who once starred in the Tarzan films. Both Peter Blake and Cheeta were born in 1932) Blake's work included several on the theme of the Madonna, placing within his paintings traditional images of the Virgin Mary in startling, modern beach settings. The pop singer, Madonna, also featured – on rollerskates!

had a disorienting and disruptive impact upon political-economic practices, the balance of class power, as well as upon cultural and social life."[19] And again he comments: "Eschewing the idea of progress, postmodernism abandons all sense of historical continuity and memory, while simultaneously developing an incredible ability to plunder history and to absorb whatever it finds there as some aspect of the present."[20]

Discontinuity with the past as well as *pessimism* about the future (both of which drive the postmodernist back on the present) are in stark contrast with the values and ethos of modernity. Rejecting strongly modernity's confident belief in inexorable progress and the prospect of utopia ahead, the postmodern spirit finds all meaning in today, in the 'now'. "Western history was universal world history...the assumption that history had an inner logic, or directional impulse, which was understood as progress...It is this assumption of a destination for history which has been most strongly challenged by...postmodern theories."[21]

In brief, social commentators have summed up the mood of post-modernity as "...modernity without the hopes and dreams that made modernity bearable."[22] In many ways it is also a return to first principles, but with a difference: "Enlightenment lifestyle without Enlightenment foundations."

The Impact Points of Postmodernity

Despite what seemed not very long ago to be its indomitable strengths, modernity is showing evident signs of succumbing to the incoming tide of postmodernity. First, knowledge is now often perceived to be piecemeal, ever changing, always beyond full reach. Even science, the favoured child of the Enlightenment, has been affected in this sense, particularly with the advent of quantum theory. Knowledge can no longer be taken for granted as objective, but is seen to be always affected by the know-er, and by the process of acquiring that knowledge.

Yet most of us have sensed all this for some time, especially if we have been part of an incident covered by the media and recorded by a TV team. What we have read or seen so often seems to us more like an interpretation of events than a description of what we for our part saw and experienced.

In the postmodern world there is no longer the conviction that knowledge is inherently:

- GOOD...a gnawing pessimism replaces the earlier optimism. No longer is there confidence that humanity will be able to solve the world's great problems, or even that the economies of the world will continue to improve from one generation to the next. Life on earth is now viewed as fragile, requiring a new attitude of cooperation rather than conquest.
- CERTAIN...and hence purely rational. The postmodern mind refuses to limit truth to its rational dimension. It recognises other paths to knowledge.
- OBJECTIVE...because the universe (multiverse?) is now not considered mechanistic and dualistic. Reality is relative, indeterminate, and participatory.

Despite the confidence of Professor Richard Dawkins, there is no longer much expectation of discovering a 'grand unified theory' that explains everything completely and perfectly.

Truth

Consequently *truth* has become much more a personal perception than a universal explanation that in time will come to be appreciated by all people

Postmodernism
An analysis by sociologist David Harvey.

"Postmodernism is difficult to pin down. Was it a style? Or a historical movement that had a definite purchase upon our imaginations for only a certain time, and only in a certain place?...it was probably both...

"So what were the elements of style?...a rejection of any over-arching propositions (theories or metanarratives or universalist styles), acceptance of pluralism and fragmentation...emphasis on difference (or otherness) and heterogeneity, and, finally, a wan or ironic admission of the ephemerality of things. As such, postmodernism defines a certain positionality...How deep this postmodern worm burrows into our subconscious and how lasting the effects might be hard to tell.

There are three levels of explanation to which we can appeal.

First, the adoption of a new position from which to argue, sketch, depict or draw the world, can be interpreted in terms of the exhaustion of, or reaction against the old...Is it not passing strange, though, that the sense of exhaustion or of some powerful urge to react against established orthodoxies should simultaneously occur in so many disciplines, and take the broadly parallel forms that they did?...

The second line of argument...attributes an across-the-board movement like modernism or postmodernism to some changing and sometimes hidden zeitgeist [spirit of the age] in the world of thought and creative endeavour.

But I think a subtler interpretation is in order...The thesis I considered in *The Condition of Postmodernity* rested primarily on an exploration of the changing experience of space and time, particularly in the period after the collapse of 1973...The definition of space and time is essential to the creation of any sense of individual or collective identity...But when these coordinates shift, become insecure, it is very hard to know who we are. What time are we in – the 24 hours of the City broker, the 100 years or so history of most nation states, or the long-term time of global warming? What space do we inhabit – the village, the nation, Europe, the West, the globe?...The search was on to reconstruct identity precisely because our positionality with respect to the world had been changed, not because we were bored with the old (though the events of 1968 suggest there was plenty of that around) but because the time and space of world affairs had shifted.

I call this kind of intensity of experience 'space-time compression'. It has happened before...Our positionality necessarily changes because the space-time coordinates of social life have become like shifting sand rather than set securely in concrete.

Postmodernism was, I would suggest, a wide-ranging set of arguments constructed in and around this background of time-space compression. The diversity of both its offerings and its critical reception have to be understood in terms of the search for identity in a world of changing space-time horizons."[23]

everywhere, equally. It is now often seen as something much more internal than external, 'truths' rather than truth. "With the collapse of grand narratives to confer privileged status on the Western tradition of the past three centuries, no single account can take priority and we are left with a conflicting field of myths and stories. There is no single truth, only truths, each for its own public and occasion in what Habermas calls 'the localisation of truth'. Knowledge becomes a commodity for chat shows. Postmodern law and justice no longer seek the unique truth but arbitrate between disjointed interest groups, each with its own truth."[24]

Pessimism has replaced optimism as to humanity's future. The 20th century artist, Francis Bacon, is an example of postmodern art. His central philosophy was that man is an accident who plays out the game of existence without reason. He dedicated himself to futility with an almost religious fervour.[25]

But during the 1980s there was also another dimension of pessimism

The Three Umpires

Three umpires compared techniques while relaxing after a game of baseball. They revealed three quite different ways of viewing the same game. The first umpire said: "There's balls and there's strikes, and I call 'em the way they are." The second umpire remarked: "There's balls and there's strikes, and I call 'em the way I see them." But the postmodern umpire said: "There's balls and there's strikes but they ain't nothin' til I call 'em"!

For the last umpire, the knowing subject's knowledge is all that there is, or all that really matters. We can never get outside our knowledge to check its accuracy against some 'objective' criterion.[26]

emerging – ecological and environmental concerns. Would our fragile planet see out many more generations the way we were using and abusing it? Some of the most ardent criticism of liberal policies concerning use of the earth and its resources during the period of modernity have come from environmentalists. David Lyon writes: "The belief that technological advancement necessarily promotes the progress of civilization is false, as the history of the 20th century attests so forcefully."[27]

Furthermore, *emotion and intuition* are increasingly replacing reason as the surest guide and the most reliable indicator of the way forward for humanity. Feelings are considered to make better sense than arguments. The advertising industry, in its reading of the postmodern condition, refers to this as 'the feel-good factor', and this plays a crucial role in determining the pitch promoters may make in their play for the attention of the consumer. Yet in areas of life that are still largely cerebral, such as the purchasing of computers and their software, the pitch is almost always to the mind, with tightly condensed descriptions of the capacities and speed potential of the PCs on offer, little hype, and no feminine figures casually draped over the monitor. The appeal is more to mental prowess and to the male desire for the most powerful machine.

Art, under the mood of postmodernity, is entered into and felt rather than observed and understood. Aesthetics rather than ethics are the principle motivator and dynamic of behaviour. Images assume greater significance than words. Some refer to this as 'logocentrism' (the centrality of the word as a means of communication) being superseded by 'iconocentrism' (the visual presentation of a message through a symbol or icon). The statement 'a good picture is worth a thousand words', however, is much older than postmodernism.

But this also means that the *spiritual dimensions* of life are now taken more seriously and encouraged. "Probably one of the most unexpected results of this changed perspective has been to revive interest in those once-tabooed aspects of otherness which can broadly be termed spiritual or religious."[28] John Drane also comments: "One of the great ironies of our time is the way that the Western Churches are declining at the same time as the sense of spiritual search in the community is increasing in intensity and fervour."[29]

There is no guarantee however that these will meekly take their cue from the Christian faith, especially if such faith is presented in a dogmatic manner, or insisted upon as having exclusive claims. "Postmodernity is more open to religious accounts than was doctrinaire modernity, but the price of such openness is to demand that all accounts relinquish their claim to transcendent unique truth."[30]

Modernity Reconsidered

Zygmunt Bauman observes: "Modernity once deemed itself *universal*. It now thinks of itself instead as *global*. Behind the change of terms hides a watershed in the history of modern self-awareness and self-confidence. Universal was to be the rule of reason – the order of things that would replace slavery to passions with the autonomy of rational beings, superstition and ignorance with truth, tribulations of the drifting plankton with self-made and thoroughly monitored history-by-design.

"Globality, in contrast, means merely that everyone everywhere may feed on McDonald's burgers and watch the latest made-for-TV docudrama. Universality was a proud project, a Herculean mission to perform. Globality,

A World Culture

Until modernity appeared, cultures were always local. But lately, modernization has been producing comparable ways of thinking, being, and wanting in countries that are very different in terms of their histories, religion and organization. Modernity has thus become culturally very thin. It can be found everywhere, but belongs nowhere. It has the habit of reducing life to clichés. And those who live by it often themselves become culturally thin people, found everywhere but belonging nowhere. They are the new 'homeless' of our societies.

in contrast, is a meek acquiescence to whatever is happening 'out there'."[31]

The rational structures that seemed to epitomise high modernity no longer carry the same weight in the emerging climate of postmodernity. An American Episcopalian study guide on the changing scene for the Anglican Church in the United States expresses this in these words: "Hierarchies are going the way of the dinosaur...Pyramids of authority are being flattened out...They are being replaced by networks...As each day passes we move irrevocably further from the familiar ordering of society we had grown used to in the forty years following World War II...As the transition to an 'information society' further accelerates, the hierarchies in Western culture that remain will crumble or disappear."

"Churches seem to find it particularly difficult to digest the implications of all that is happening, and to adjust their denominational structures accordingly...Generations of pyramid-style authority structures do not disappear overnight...Babyboomers who came to adulthood in the 1960s and early 1970s grew up with the assumption that no leader is above reproof, and that all leaders should be kept under constant scrutiny...There is a subconscious distrust of those in authority – even their own peers. They want power bases to be broad, lines of authority short, and they expect a high degree of accountability. Networks suit their *modus vivendi* admirably. ...They get impatient with unwieldy, inflexible organisations that are not designed to listen and respond to the grass roots...[They are] more likely to feel that if they cannot have 'hands on' involvement then they are not interested in being involved at all."[32]

This reducing to size of the universal illusions of grandeur entertained by modernity was evident not only in the lower profile of the United Nations through the last two decades of the century, but also in the decline of the role and presence of the World Council of Churches over this same time.

This sense of progressing towards an eventual global Christianity that would be expressed in "the coming great Church" was not exclusive to the modernist vision of post-World War II ecumenical enthusiasts. Well before this period, as far back as 1930, Anglican bishops were supporting a point of view that stated: "...in its present character we believe that the Anglican Communion is transitional, and we forecast the day when the racial and historical connections which at present characterise it will be transcended and the life of our communion will be merged in a larger fellowship in the Catholic Church."[33]

Behind much of this surge towards a world Church was not only a spirit of modernity that fitted those times, but also some of the theological legacy of the Enlightenment with its emphasis on the rational. Lesslie Newbigin, himself a stalwart of the world ecumenical movement in his day, caustically comments: " 'The larger ecumenism' is a phrase used to describe what is really only an expression of religious relativism, the goal of all world religions moving towards a universal fellowship in which all will respect the truth of the others. What is proposed is to relativize the significance of Jesus Christ as Son of God and Saviour of the world. It is the triumph of relativism over truth. It is a neo-imperialism in the interests of certain people. It is a disastrous error to set universalism against the concrete particularity of what God has done for the whole creation in Jesus Christ."[34]

Rather than herald an end-times explosion of Christian belief and church life in the Western world as modernity reached its apex, the opposite occurred. Over the period of the 1960s-1990s church membership in the West declined dramatically. But paradoxically, as has already been noted, openness to the spiritual continued. It simply retreated to the world of leisure time and personal options, and it declined to commit itself to any one camp. Andrew Walker observes: "Religiosity has not disappeared, it has been relocated to the private sphere of cultural existence. Christianity in particular has either voluntarily decamped from the 'public square', or been forcibly removed from it to the private world."[35]

Modernism in sociology and in theology had predicated a future that could only get better and better. This was based on two assumptions: first, the inherent natural goodness and perfectibility of humankind; second, the extension of an advanced theory of evolution to embrace the development of human character. But even sharp antagonists of a Christian worldview such as Richard Dawkins argued that from the point of view of biology we are at bottom nasty, "inescapably selfish."[36]

In summary, the *goals of modernity* were:

- *a flat earth* – no transcendence; flattened authority structures.
- *a real life* – authentic individual personhood; open societies.
- *a great future* – confidence in human ability; inevitable progress through science and education.
- *a universal vision* – United Nations Organization/World Council of Churches; a world order organised for peace.

But in the end this created a public climate that left little room for God. On the other hand, the *impact of postmodernity* seems more likely to be:

- *uncertainty* – a more tentative and humbler attitude to the future.[37]
- *spirituality* – greater openness to the spiritual dimensions of life.
- *diversity* – aversion to 'the scandal of particularity' e.g. metanarrative.
- *locality* – value of the indigenous culture and natural environment.

This creates a climate in which there is again room for God – but also openness to other competing claimants for the tenancy of this space to let – and a reluctance of the lessors to agree to *any* long term leases to *anyone*.

Contrasting the eras of the *premodern, modern,* and *postmodern* worlds, and their **prevailing images**, it may be said:

- The *pre-modern* world = organic and hierarchical.
- The *modern* world = rational and mechanical.[38]
- The *postmodern* world = relational, personal and approximate.

James B. Miller describes *the postmodern worldview* with its tentativeness thus:

- *The world is evolutionary*: i.e., always becoming, changing, developing. It has no fixed or eternal essence determining its form.
- *Humanity is only a feature of creation*: i.e., not necessarily the final crown.
- *Creation may be insubstantial*: i.e., composed rather of dynamic relationships than of fixed matter. So we have the benefit of the insights of quantum physics.
- *The inherent principle of uncertainty is at the heart of the universe*: i.e., no amount or quality of observation can conclude the real. At the core of reality there is always mystery.
- *The future is indeterminable*: i.e., you can only be sure of probable results; no one can be dogmatic about any outcome of even the most assured scientific process.
- *There are no such things as objective facts*: i.e., except within a community where an agreed discipline of knowing and describing is accepted. There can ever only be relative objectivity because the very process of observing adds a variable to any situation.[39]

Architectural Changes of Postmodernity

Visually the impact of postmodernity is to be seen most of all in the changes reflected in architectural design, especially over the last two decades of the 20th century. For example, when a terrorist bomb destroyed a large part of the commercial centre of Manchester in 1995, it presented the city with the opportunity to rebuild the heart of the city in such a way as to minimize the visual impact of the unattractive and unloved Arndale Centre. Yet in the 1970s when this high-rise commercial block was constructed, it was considered to be a prime example of the modernist architecture of that period, a monument to progress.

But as early as the same 1970s some architects were questioning the shaping of their goals under modernity. A group of architects writing in 1972 (*Learning From Las Vegas*) expressed this conviction. It was time, they said, to build for people rather than for Man!

David Harvey in his book, *The Condition of Postmodernity*, puts it this way: "The glass towers, concrete blocks, and steel slabs that seemed set fair to steamroller over every urban landscape from Paris to Tokyo and from Rio to Montreal, denouncing all ornament as crime, all individualism as sentimentality, all romanticism as kitsch, have progressively given way to ornamented tower blocks, imitation medieval squares and fishing villages, customer designed or vernacular housing, renovated factories and warehouses, and rehabilitated landscapes of all kinds, all in the name of procuring some more 'satisfying' urban environment. So popular has this quest become that no less a figure than Prince Charles has weighed in with vigorous denunciations of the errors of post-war urban redevelopment and the developer destruction that has done more to wreck London, he claims, than the Luftwaffe's attacks in World War II."[40]

CHAPTER FIVE

Postmodernity
and the Consumer Society

The Pervasiveness of Postmodernity

Like an incoming tide, postmodernity is progressively and relentlessly encroaching on to more and more areas of Western culture. Take, for example, *the arts*. Mike Featherstone writes: "Among the central features associated with postmodernism in the arts are: the effacement of the boundary between art and everyday life; the collapse of the hierarchical distinction between high and mass/popular culture; a stylistic promiscuity favouring eclecticism and the mixing of codes; parody, pastiche, irony, playfulness and the celebration of the surface 'depthlessness' of culture; the decline of the originality/genius of the artistic producer; and the assumption that art can only be repetition."[1]

A principle of *modernist art* is stylistic integrity. In contrast *postmodern art* embraces stylistic diversity, or 'multivalence'. A favoured form of composition is the collage which Jacques Derrida describes as "the primary form of postmodern discourse." Postmodern art emphasizes process and production, it may even be incomplete, inviting the viewer into the work. It will often employ juxtaposition of images – to barrage the viewer with incongruous, even clashing pieces. It is frequently disjointed, offering an unharmonious pastiche with gaudy colour schemes and discordant typography.

This style is now moving out of high culture and finding its way on to book dust covers, into advertising, on to the TV screen. It was noticeably a feature of the Monty Python show. Whether knowingly or not, it is often today the style by which contemporary youth promote their activities. Pub posters may take this form. In London, the *The Times* produces a weekly insert, 'Young Times', that has this feel about it. In contrast, the newspaper that enfolds it has all the characteristics of modernity – carefully measured, column-like format with a centred illustration related to the feature article on that front page. In New Zealand the same contrast can be seen in comparing the weekly 'classroom' supplement in some dailies with the rest of the paper.

Architecture tells the same story. Until the 1970s *modernism* dominated building design and produced the 'International Style', fashioned by a confident faith in human rationality and high hopes of achieving a human utopia. The principle of unity determined design, each building intended to express one unified, essential meaning. Thus modern buildings are often characterised by simple, unitary forms, nearly always expressed in some sort of glass and steel box. New Zealand architects, at home or abroad, were at one stage particularly prone to producing this style, thus providing significant 'signature buildings' of the late modern period. New Zealand House in the Haymarket, London, and the State Insurance building in Christchurch's Cathedral Square, are prime examples of this.

Architecture need not necessarily be unattractive in its functional austerity. The design of the Guggenheim Museum in New York bears this out. But postmodernist architects reject this modernist concept as too austere. Their works, such as Lloyds Insurance building, London, and the Pompidou Centre, Paris, purposely explore and display incompatibilities of style, form and texture. "Postmoderns complain that none of the architectural wonders of the past, such as the great Cathedrals which point to another realm, could have been built during the reign of modernism."[2] Modernist architect Mies van der Rohe in the 1920s wrote: "Architecture is the will of the age conceived in spatial terms."[3] The Prince of Wales refers to 'carbuncles' on the face of the city, meaning (to his mind) the monstrosities of modernity!

Film and television provide another area where the incoming tide of post-modernity can be discerned. Living today in a postmodern society, so largely conditioned by television and mesmerised by the lure of the big screen, means inhabiting a film-like world – a realm in which truth and fiction meet. Virtual Reality. 'Faction'. This merges the real into the fantasy, and conveys a sense of the fantasy really being the real. But often all that such experience does is to open a window into the mind of the producer – for those who are able to see through it. TV has globally infected the modern world with the postmodern virus. It has become the real world and source of truth for a new generation, blurring the line between truth and fiction, between the truly earth-shattering and the trivial. By giving roughly equal treatment to a variety of images in quick succession, news stories and commercials alike, broadcasts leave the impression that these are all of roughly equal importance.

More than that, TV also offers an increasing choice of programmes. "A viewer can shuttle through the wasteland perpetually in search of something interesting...Television intrinsically displays what some critics see as two central characteristics of postmodern texts: it effaces the boundary between past and present, and it locates the viewer in a perpetual present."[4]

Then there is *pop culture*. One consequence of the impact of post-modernity has been the demolition of the wall between high culture and mass culture. Traditional barriers, lines of demarcation, class and social cultural divisions have all been eroded – in terms of taste, participation, defined territories, and even the dress of those who participate. Artists and musicians, painters and wordsmiths, are all likely to be found immersed in the activities of what, under modernity, would have been recognised widely as differentiated and segregated areas of culture. Pop culture has invaded high society. High culture has taken to the streets. The seduction of the advertising industry, with its endless dollars to spend, and its attractions of freedom for creative film-making and publicity design work, has brought the best of skills and the breadth of culture into everyday life – and this is by no means bad. David Harvey writes: "Whatever else we do with the concept, we should not read postmodernism as some autonomous artistic current. Its rootedness in daily life is one of its most patently transparent features."[5]

The attitudes and values of the new generation also reflect this invasion of the familiar world of the past. Yet all this has been at a price. The cost has been the sense of security of identity both of the individual and of the local community. This was an assumed feature of older societies, even up until late modernity, held in place by the scaffolding of ancient traditions, hierarchies, community values and faith. Now disturbing numbers of people in the Western world, especially those on the threshold of life, are showing symptoms of unprecedented stress – eating disorders, mental illnesses, youth suicides, drug dependency, mindless vandalism, domestic violence. Too many of this generation have too little idea of who they are, or to what family of people they belong. "People no longer know where the lines fall...With the help of plastic surgeons and make-up artists, Michael Jackson continues to look more like his sister. Our computers are starting to talk to us while our neighbours are becoming more distant and anonymous...The new eugenics seem to be saying that human beings – especially those at the peripheries of life, the unborn and the aged – do not have hearts or minds worth worrying about."[6]

Will the promise of maturity of character and outlook through celebration of diversity upon which postmodernity is premised be fulfilled as society passes through this transition period? Or are we asking too much of the human person, without also providing a compensatory social framework to enable all to live so loosely? Under late modernity there was great confidence in the inherent strength of the autonomous individual to cope on their own with any kind of change. Postmodernity has dispelled that myth.

But there is also wide agreement that there is no going back to what we were before the bubble of modernity burst. Some speak of modernity wearing itself out, forgetting its lofty goals. "Western civilization suffers from a strong sense of moral and spiritual exhaustion. Having constructed a society of unprecedented sophistication, convenience and prosperity, nobody can

The Chimera of Postmodernity

"Postmodern disciplines and discourses continually destabilize the process of representation by a variety of tropes: irony, quotation, parody, stylistic promiscuity, eclecticism, pastiche, jokeyness and playfulness, all aimed at distancing the reader or viewer from the representation. Thus postmodern design uses different typefaces and irregular left margin; film, a variety of visual references to different periods, genres and classic films; architecture, an eclectic mix of styles and decorative reference ironically juxtaposed; and literature, a plethora of genre, style, temporal reference and typography.

Each in its own way makes the point that there is no fixed point of reference, no object world outside of representation, no knowledge of this world, and that style is nine points of the real...We now have a surface of representations, without depth and without differentiation. Postmodernity celebrates surface over depth and transforms into the figural, into images. Visual images are privileged over words; the immersion of the spectator over the objectivity of the observer."[7]

remember what it was supposed to be for."[8] Whither then this new generation and the society in which they will grow old?

The Overlap of Modernity with Postmodernity

When a major culture shift takes place such as we are beginning to witness in the West, it is not like a change of government or a political revolution. The process is unpredictable and variable, overlapping wavelets of change like the incoming tide on a long, gently shelving beach; at this point advancing, at that point seeming to recede. But the movement over a long period of time is still unmistakable, even if its immediate pattern is unclear to the eye.

Andrew Walker writes of the difficulty of "assessing the significance of contemporary change [when you are living in the midst of it]. It is only with hindsight that we can safely say that we have passed from one era to another,

Television has a lot to answer for

"The saturation of our culture with this new technology has had an effect on the development of the modern consciousness as profound and pervasive as that of the printing press in Europe centuries ago. Ours is now the first generation whose daily experience is both shared and interpreted through a single medium to which people in the West...are exposed for a considerable period of their waking hours."[9] Television is the voice of our world cliché culture.

David Wells

or that our culture used to be that but now is this. Furthermore, a culture does not cease to exist by rational decree or through prophetic punditry: It lingers on until it eventually becomes absorbed into the new one or atrophies. Feudalism, for example, did not suddenly disappear with the birth of capitalism in the Protestant countries of 16th century Europe. On the contrary, life for the European peasant in the 17th century was little different from peasant life in the 7th century...Cultural change, even when it is as rapid as the transition of Tsarist Russia to the Soviet Union, is a matter of continuities with the old order as well as discontinuities."[10]

And there is always the confusion caused by living in such a time of transition. As David Bosch sees it: "New paradigms do not establish themselves overnight. They take decades, sometimes even centuries, to develop distinctive contours. The new paradigm is therefore still emerging and it is as yet not clear which shape it will eventually adopt. For the most part we are, at the moment, thinking and working in terms of *two* paradigms...A time of paradigm shift is a time of deep uncertainty."[11] We are living in such a time now. Features of high modernity continue to abound around us, even vestiges still of a premodern age, especially in ancient institutions and powerful centres of learning such as Oxford and Cambridge Universities that have been able to withstand many of the ravages of successive culture changes over the centuries.

In a personal testimony to this unease, David Wells says with feeling: "Since our intellectual world has died, modern life is being defined more by its social processes and cultural environment and less by any ideology. Ideas have largely lost the power to shape life. The human spirit is now being moved not by profound thinking but by the experience of living in a metropolis presided over by bureaucracy, tranquillized by television, and awash with the racket of clashing cultures...The benefits of modern life are undeniable...It is the deceptions of modernity I reject."[12]

Some of the features, then, that were such distinguishing marks of modernity at its height continue to exercise a dominating role in shaping the world about us.

In the confusions that inevitably accompany transition, the arts can prove to be surprisingly accurate indicators of where in another decade most of society may be, rather than simply serving as mirrors held up to current society. And such times of transition will bring possibilities of both gains and losses for the Christian faith in Western societies as postmodernity impacts upon communities whose faith had once been so firmly bedded in the premodern, and then so largely conditioned by the modern.

Pausing to Evaluate

Some read the signs of postmodernity as evidence of a quest to move beyond modernity, as a need to find a new paradigm for understanding and living in our world. Others interpret what is happening as modernity being taken to a greater depth, as simply an extension of modernity, but at a new level. Anthony Giddens, for example, writes: "Rather than entering a period of postmodernity, we are moving into one in which the consequences of modernity are becoming more and more radicalized and universalized than ever before." Giddens describes this as a 'discontinuist' view of modern social development, having little if any relationship to previous ways of ordering society. His contribution is primarily in the area of institutional change. He would prefer to think of current changes taking place as 'radicalized modernity', or 'high modernity', rather than 'postmodernity'.[13]

Such social commentators might describe these times therefore as 'high modernity', rather than a period following modernity. Thus Thomas Oden favours the term 'ultra-modern' or even 'postcritical' to describe his perception of these changes: "What is named post is actually a desperate extension of despairing modernity." He also refers to this as 'terminal modernity'. In the end he concedes the usefulness of the term 'postmodernity', even with its ambiguous assumptions and shortcomings.[14] But others believe that what we are witnessing will in the end come to be seen as a wholesale rejection of modernity, with postmodernity as a new era.

Another possible way of describing these times that does justice to both a sense of continuity and the radical change of life this entails, is to speak of the period as 'modernity in menopause'. Thomas Oden later comments: "Modernity is not dead in the sense that all its repercussions and consequences are over, but in the sense that the ideological engine propelling the movement of modernity is broken down irreparably."[15] For many this may bring more regrets than rejoicing as the climate of Western societies steadily changes in its philosophical temperature.

"You will arise and have mercy on Jerusalem:
for the time has come to pity her.
Even her tumbled stones are dear to your servants:
it moves them with pity to see her in the dust."

Psalm 102: 13-14, *A New Zealand Prayer Book*

In considering the relationship of modernity to postmodernity (indeed, even these two to premodern times) as a paradigm shift, the analogy of roading in Britain may help. Ermine Street is today an important route from Lincoln to the Humber, extending in an almost straight line for over twenty miles. For the most part it follows and is built upon the ancient Roman road of that name and route. Roadmakers over subsequent centuries did not see reason in this instance to divert from the course and foundations laid down by the Roman occupation in the early centuries of the Christian era.

Yet from generation to generation this same road has been overlaid with new and more suitable surfaces for changed conditions and needs of travel. But, in addition, down the ages many other new roads and motorways have also been developed where no previous road existed. In some situations old patterns of roading were followed, usually enlarged and greatly improved, but these deviated where they no longer served the best interests of travellers. Others were entirely new routes cut savagely through ancient farmlands and forests. Many of the older roading systems are now entirely lost. They had outlived their usefulness.

So the transition from one paradigm to another may not entail the immediate or wholesale discarding of all the old ways of the previous paradigm. Some of the premodern still remains with us centuries later, and is alive and well today (for example, Gregorian chants, the Book of Common Prayer, elements of ecclesiastical robes and rituals, academic traditions in the Colleges of Oxbridge, etc.). So the modern is also likely to persist long into future generations in many forms. But, like crossing the equator, gradually – even rapidly if you are a jet traveller – the climate will be found to be increasingly different. Society, one discovers, is living according to another paradigm. The sun is in a different part of the sky.

Impact on Modernity

Modernity was in incubation for more than a hundred years before emerging from its womb with the labour pains of the Industrial Revolution. This was then followed by a lengthy period of awkward adolescence lasting more than another hundred years before modernity finally this century found its full maturity in the turbulent decade of the 1960s. Postmodernity, on the other hand, seems more likely to be remembered for the rapidity with which it is now developing and the suddenness with which it is emerging as a further new paradigm.

The principle challenges that postmodernity poses to key tenets of modernity lie in the areas of modernity's confidence in rationality, its belief in progress, its reliance on metanarratives, its fixation on the centrality of the self, its ambitions of universality, its dependence upon science, and its optimism concerning the future.

Confidence in the controlling powers of **rationality** was often at the expense of respect for other facets of our humanity. One can be critical of the excessive dependence in our immediate past on rational processes to address all situations, meet all needs and solve all problems, without at the same time having to discard the contribution of reason to our search for a more holistic approach to life and experience of reality. "This is our fate: to reconcile the demands of rationality and those of the sublime."[16]

Reliance on the grand story, **the metanarrative**, to account for our meaning and significance was not rejected by modernity. On the contrary, it was a case of one grand story, the story told in the Hebrew and Christian Scriptures, being replaced by another. It is postmodernity that rejects them all. "The modern outlook claims to have replaced myths with rational postulates, but postmodern thinkers assert that the Enlightenment project is itself dependent on an appeal to narrative...The modern era viewed itself as the embodiment of a narrative of progress – a myth that legitimated technological invention and economic development as the means of creating a better world for all human beings. For a time, this story was challenged by a variant – the Marxist narrative of an inevitable revolution that would lead to the utopia of international socialism. But at no point, say the postmoderns, did moderns ever really free themselves from the directive force of myth... What makes our condition 'postmodern' is not only that people no longer cling to the myths of modernity. The postmodern outlook entails the end of the appeal to any central legitimating myth whatsoever...Consequently, the postmodern outlook demands an attack on any claimant to universality – it demands, in fact, a 'war on totality'."[17]

Yet there is an inconsistency in this rejection of overarching theories. Critics argue that the often quoted conclusion of Jean-Francois Lyotard in *The Postmodern Condition* in which he said: "*Simplifying to the extreme, I define postmodern as incredulity toward metanarratives.*" itself entails a master narrative, and that you cannot have a theory of the postmodern without one.

Modernity's narcissistic *preoccupation with the 'self'* has also been subject to challenge arising out of the new mood of postmodernity. If the *modern* autonomous self sought to dominate the world, convinced of an ideal of universal, rational progress, the *postmodern* self vacillates between a new form of autonomy and a sense of victimization. A product of a disillusioned modernism, the postmodern self finds itself in "a contradictory state of possessing an insatiable desire for all the smorgasbord of riches life has to offer while feeling overcome by a sense of meaninglessness, powerlessness, rootlessness, homelessness, and fragmentation...The 'I want it all' attitude is easily transmuted into the 'I'm paralysed in the face of it all.' The postmodern self thus exists in a perpetual state of dialectical self-contradiction."[18]

The **universalism** of modernity, with its aspirations for one world order, has also lost credibility in the increasingly postmodern climate at the end of the 20th century. Centrelessness is a feature of postmodernity. No longer are there common standards to which all conform more or less, whether in dress, lifestyle, ideas, values, or building designs. Gone as well are the old allegiances to a common source of authority. The dream of moving towards a *utopia* has been replaced by the reality of this postmodern *heterotopia*, the 'multiverse' that has replaced the 'universe' of modernity's hopes and aspirations. Hans Bertens refers to the way "in which the politics of difference and identity are replacing the former politics of repressive unity."[19]

Finally, modernity's dependence upon **science**, and an optimism concerning the future that this induced, has suffered a body blow under the forces of postmodernity. "The breakdown of the scientific worldview is more curious than it appears. It is not because it has been replaced by religion, or any other worldview for that matter. It is certainly not because there are no more frontiers left to conquer...Quite simply, science has been subsumed under functional rationality. It is no longer viewed as an independent activity, intrinsically good in itself. Instead, science has become the handmaiden of government, industry, commerce, private laboratories working in the commercial field, and the leisure industry. Increasingly scientists have become adjuncts of the market. Pure research no longer stands out as innovative, daring or ground-breaking. We might say that the intelligentsia has caught up with the view that the general public has held for years: science is technology and skilful technique that achieves marvellous things.

"We do not know for sure, but it seems likely that the disenchantment with science is part of the decline in the plausibility of all metanarratives."[20]

Alongside these shifts in values and perceptions another major change was taking place. The Protestant work ethic of the regime of modernity became, under the emancipating influence of postmodernity, a post-Christendom leisure ethic.[21] In the words of one sociologist: "If postmodernity means anything, it means the consumer society."[22] It has been suggested that Descartes', *Cogito, ergo sum,* might today be better expressed as *Tesco, ergo sum.* For many contemporaries, the shopping mall has become the temple you flee to for relief when life is getting you down. But not for all, as Middleton and Walsh see it: "Shopping when you know exactly what you need and where to get it is often an enjoyable, even relaxing, experience. Aimlessly wandering through a mall with an incredible range of consumer options can be extremely tiring. It is not the multiplicity of options that exhausts us; at bottom it is the inability to make a normative choice."

The Consumer Society

There was a growing awareness through the 1990s of the significance of consumerism as a new factor in the onslaught on modernity: "... consumerism and mass culture, which began in the 1950s, have arguably changed the nature of modernity, paving the way for its dissolution or disappearance as a cultural era."[23] This was a development that on first appearance had little obvious connection with the ideas and ideals of postmodernity, but on closer examination reflected many of its emerging features, whether as a consequence of or as a contribution to postmodernity. It was an example of similar reactive responses to magisterial modernity that arose during the '80s and '90s at different points in Western society, without seeming collaboration or design.

Consumerism arose once the successes of first the industrial revolution and then the technological revolution created more goods than were necessary to meet the immediate needs of available markets. While for many years there always existed the possibility of discovering fresh markets for the sale of these goods, such openings were limited. The answer was to move from the meeting of natural needs in new markets to the creation of new needs within existing markets; to change purchasing in order to live into buying as a way of life. So the consumer society was born.

The Birth of Consumerism in the 1950s

"The defining moment in modernity, when it passed from its early to its late phase, was not the permissive 1960s, or the microchip wizardry of the 1990s, but the burgeoning consumption of the 1950s."[24] "Beginning in the United States, and heralded in the 1940s by Henry Ford, consumerism has become the dominant cultural force of the last half of the century. 'Fordism' was the application of mechanical mass-production methods to create consumer durables for a mass public at affordable and competitive prices. This 'Fordism', with its skilled workforce, paved the way for the first phase of the consumer society...

"To register the dream-like quality of the 1950s is important, because it demonstrates that right from the beginning, the consumer revolution was predicated not only upon a built-in obsolescence of consumer durables, but also on the fact that selling goods was the selling of a life-style. Consumer goods were not value-free, but came packaged with an association of ideas.[25]

"Before the 1950s were over, people had learned to buy products because they were thought to be good in themselves, enhanced a desired lifestyle, and were associated with a favourite film, television programme, or famous personality. It was as if the glamour and fame of the 'stars' could rub off on you like pixie dust when you bought products tagged to their names." In the consumer society everything is marketed as a commodity to satisfy some internal dissatisfaction – sex, comfort, security, even knowledge. "Our commerce, it has been said, has become our culture, and advertising is the art form that weaves them together."[26]

The selling of image is also big business. Christopher Lasch suggests that the development of the postmodern personality is rooted in the slow disintegration of the family that began at least a hundred years ago.

Lasch reasons that this has led to producing the 'narcissistic' personality, by which he means a person who has been hollowed out and evacuated of the internal moral gyroscope of character belonging to former generations.

Instead, an exaggerated interest in image as opposed to substance has produced a personality that is typically shallow, self-absorbed, elusive, leery of commitments, unattached to people or place, dedicated to keeping all options open, and frequently incapable of either loyalty or gratitude.[27]

Consumption has been around for a long time, but under modernity and the triumph of Enlightenment ideals, this took place in a context of morality, justice, rationality, confidence in progress, etc. But these meta-narratives have vanished. It was modernity which severed the high ground from its moorings in God – and once cut loose, the lingering values realized their nakedness and ran for cover. Today we are left with no recognised values, little arguable rationality.

So the postmodern mood is essentially nihilistic. "It wanders the world blankly, no longer looking for meaning...it lives for the surface and abjures what lies beneath. It views a search for depth and meaning as nostalgic, a longing for a world now lost forever." Postmodernity in this sense is unrestrained modernity, released from the values and restraints of the past. The consumer society not only provides the range of goods and an accessibility to them that sustains the new industry of purchasing alongside the business of manufacturing, it also elevates the promotion of products and the experience of selecting purchases into a high art. The object is to convince the public that today's luxuries are tomorrow's necessities. (Check this out within our own domestic experience: a refrigerator, a telephone in the home, a TV, hi-fi stereo, CD player, microwave, personal computer, etc.) And in societies where consumption is king, continual development and promotion of the new and the better is vital. Production bows down to promotion.

So a new art-form is born, and the advertising industry takes on a life and a meaning of its own. The outcomes are significant:

- The presentation of goods is determined as much by aesthetic considerations as by functional. Window dressing and display stand decoration become arts in their own right.
- Shopping (often only window shopping) becomes a leisure pursuit enjoyed for itself. And leisure increasingly for many becomes their 'realizable utopia'. But, writes Christopher Lasch, "it is misleading to

characterize the culture of consumption as a culture dominated by things. The consumer lives surrounded not so much by things as by fantasies. He lives in a world that has no objective or independent existence and seems to exist only to gratify or thwart his desires."

- Closed-in shopping centres, all-embracing in what they offer and the services they provide (under cover free parking, food halls, one-stop shopping) replace the local corner stores and family firms where our parents first brought us shopping.

- New levels of co-operation, both with fellow tenants of the shopping precinct and also with city planners, enable malls or neighbourhood commercial developments to extend their services to sponsoring concerts and entertainment under their roof, to promoting street activities and the revival of historic features of the city's past. In Christchurch, New Zealand, old trams have been brought out of retirement and given a fresh set of tracks and a route that winds through cultural and commercial areas of the city. They are enjoyed and used by citizens and tourists alike.

- For some families, the weekend visit to the shopping mall (which may well be the highlight of their Sunday) is also the nearest they get to a regular religious observance. It is something they can do together, there is no compulsion to buy, entertainment is often provided, they meet other people with similar interests, they are left with a feeling of well-being from the experience. David Wells relates the way of life of the citizens of Wenham, Massachusetts, 200 years ago: "When our Wenham townswoman became depressed she would have gone into the church to pray; her counterpart today would probably go to the mall to shop."[28] 'Retail therapy' has worked its miracle; 'image' has left its mark.

One comment on the U.S. scene suggests that: "Malls are the cathedrals of late modernity, where people come to gaze and wonder in the sacred space, to offer homage and pay their dues to the gods of mammon. In Dallas, Texas, one major Baptist Church has been built to look like a mall, and has created space to 'hang out' and shop in, as well as providing sanctuaries for worship."[29] The same sense of sacred space can be applied to a new concept of shopping centres being proposed in a small nation on the other side of the world such as New Zealand. For example, in 1997 land was being purchased in a number of centres across the nation for the creation of a chain of 60,000 square metre shopping malls that would make even the existing mega-malls in this country seem insignificant. Writing about these proposals the investigative journalist said: "They are our consumer temples. They are clean, well lit, warm, safe. The shops are modern, nicely designed. There's entertainment, a sense of scale, even of occasion. They smell good."[30]

But there are also wider ramifications to this spirit of consumerism. Consumer culture can be summarised as:

- Needs will always be met and matched by products.
- Personal desires of the consumer are top priority.
- Choice must always be available.
- Brand change is acceptable.

"Once established, such a culture of consumption is quite undiscriminating and everything becomes a consumer item, including meaning, truth and knowledge."[31] "Knowledge itself becomes a key commodity, to be produced and sold to the highest bidder, under conditions that are themselves increasingly organised on a competitive basis."[32]

Palmerston North, New Zealand, is a small city of some 77,000 population, of whom 12.5 percent are directly involved in the knowledge industry. Massey University is a dominant presence in the community. The City Corporation, in setting out its Five Year Plan for the development of the city, draws attention to this asset in its midst of "commercially prized knowledge", and the primacy of this asset in the future of the city. In other parts of the Western world, other small cities with universities market themselves in similar fashion.

The consumer society becomes a world where choice is taken for granted, where variety is the spice of life, inspection without commitment to purchase is assumed, and pleasure rather than production is the way of living. This attitude often seeps into the Church – how it offers its goods, how people can inspect them, and the context of pleasurable entertainment in which this must take place – without any pressure to commitment.[33]

We are now in a religious market economy. "The church growth movement and some evangelistic crusades have accommodated to these social changes by marketing the Gospel as a product for today's postmodern consumer; spectacle and image displace explanation and word; the service style is carefully matched to consumer preference; and the message is tailored to chime with felt needs, carefully excluding discomforting feelings."[34] The pluralist situation is, above all, a *market situation*. In it, the religious institutions become marketing agencies and the religious traditions become consumer commodities.[35]

From the Supermarket to the Personal Computer

The modern era has been labelled the industrial age because of its domination by manufacturing and its focus on the production of goods. Its symbol was the factory. At its highest point of development, in the period we sometimes refer to as late modernity, this focus shifted to the consumption of goods and its symbols now became the supermarket and the shopping mall.

The postmodern era, in contrast, focuses on the production of information. So from the beginning of the 1980s Western societies have been in the throes of transition from an industrial society to an information society,[36] the symbol of which is the computer. (As early as the late 1970s, only 13 percent of American workers were still involved in the manufacture of goods, whereas already by that time 60 percent had become engaged in the manufacture of information!)

Previously information could spread no faster than human beings could travel. More significant today than speedier and cheaper travel is the modern capability to acquire and transmit information from almost anywhere to almost everywhere in the world, almost instantaneously. This in turn has led to an increasing sense of:

- being citizens of the world,
- the cultural diversity of our planet,
- the need for a pluralist mindset that appreciates and affirms difference,
- a demand for a new style of life – eclecticism – the style of postmodernity.

(We are moving away from the mass culture of modernity, that offered a few styles within a uniform range related to the seasons, toward a fragmented 'taste culture' that offers an almost endless variety of styles. Hence the announcement by one of the world's leading couturiers at a fashion show in Paris in 1996 that "fashion is out" – henceforth his great fashion house would not be dictating colours and styles for a new season!)

Many are coming to see this kind of lifestyle as reality turning in on itself, as a neglect of the ends for the means, a reality created and controlled (even if for good) by managers for their own purposes. Yet increasingly this seems to represent the 'reality' of postmodernity. It is, in effect, the creation of a 'disposable society'. "The media will produce the images and change at a regular rate in order to provide us with styles to consume and identities to try out...both styles and identities are disposable. This is the ultimate irony of the disposable society of advanced capitalism. Whatever is mastered, constructed and produced is, in the end, disposable – even identities!"[37]

The Information Age

The spread of postmodernism parallels and has been greatly dependent on the transition to an information society. (It is significant to note that the microchip made its entry on to the communications stage in 1971.)

As early as 1967 Marshall McLuhan, in a prescient insight into the way the future was shaping, wrote: "The medium or process of our time – electronic technology – is reshaping and restructuring patterns of social interdependence and every aspect of our personal life. It is forcing us to reconsider and re-evaluate practically every thought, every action and institution formerly taken for granted. Everything is changing, you, your family, your education, your neighbourhood, your government, your relation to 'the others'; and they're changing rapidly."

Information technology has enlarged human experience while shrinking the world. In 1874 my Carrell forebears took over three months (102 days) to sail from Gravesend to New Zealand. Now a flight with a brief transit pause in Singapore or Los Angeles takes their descendants just under 24 hours to cover the same distance (even less if they were able to fly by

Cyberspace

'Cyberspace' as a word in popular use has now moved out of the realms of science fiction and become a technical term in the classroom. It speaks of a new dimension to human experience that can now be accessed via the Internet. By the end of 1996, 'hits' by Internet users in the Western world were increasing at an average rate of 10,000 per day. In the six months July 1995-January 1996, Internet host computer connections increased in the United kingdom by 55 percent, Australia by 49 percent, the USA by 42 percent, and New Zealand by 22 percent.[38]

Concorde). A single exchange of mail between New Zealand and Great Britain in the 1870s took a minimum of six months. Today their descendants exchange multiple messages by email in a matter of minutes. One family member, whose work takes him constantly around the world in an irregular pattern, can just as easily and quickly pick up his business or domestic email in Los Angeles, London, Frankfurt, Tokyo, Sydney – or at his home in the South Island.

"This is indeed the annihilation of space", was an early press comment made on advances in communications technology. Surprisingly, this referred not to late 20th century email and voice mail, but to an observation recorded in the *Baltimore Patriot* in May 1844, about the significance of Morse telegraph communications! In this respect information technology both signalled the supreme success of modernity while also triggering its progressive demise. Francis Bacon claimed at the birth of modernity, "knowledge is power." The Enlightenment took knowledge out of the cloister and placed it in the hands of the savant and the scientist, thus destroying the hegemony of the Church. Information technology takes knowledge out of the hands of the learned and the literate, the maestros of modernity, and places it in the personal computers of the public, thus undercutting the very powerbrokers of modernity. By 1996, 27.6 percent of New Zealand households had at least one personal computer. There were 174,000 computers connected to the

Internet in a nation with a population of only 3.6 million. By early 1998, almost 10,000 New Zealand organizations had either web or email connections. Twelve months previously there had only been 6000.[39] And yet in one paradoxical sense such technology is an extension of modernity, because at its heart still is technical reason – except now it is digitally encoded.

So the *information superhighway* (or *infobahn*) takes over as the significant technology of the 'information revolution'. The barriers have been broached. The cyberspace of information, awash with cyberjunk, is there for the taking.

Virtual Reality

Or, if the viewer wishes, there is the opportunity to link up with others in order to shape one's own virtual universe, using the Internet with its own 'qwerty sign and shorthand language', and distinguished by an absence of international barriers, hierarchies, authorities, social distinctions, commitments, and demands. A world of postmodernity on our desktop.

"All this challenges the conventional notion – common to many moderns and Christians – that a single universe exists out there, independent of our perception. Reality is not what it used to be, and now electronics, not just drugs, offer entry into virtuality."[40]

French sociologist, Jean Baudrillard, claims that electronic culture has altered the nature of reality by creating 'a seduction of simulation' through uses of image and sign that are more human perceptions, lending an air of reality, than bridges to a reality beyond the image itself. Hence 'virtual reality'. This has also been described as 'hyperreality', where images overcome objects in the world, and suggest a reality more real than the real. Baudrillard devised the term 'simulacrum' (shadowy deceptions that refer to nothing but themselves) to describe this.[41]

For Baudrillard, the primary function of consumer items is their function as signs. This is promoted by life-style advertisements, television commercial images, and larger than life advertising hoardings, all persuading us to invest in these items. The product is invariably supported by association with a person, an activity, a set of desirable objects, that tell us: 'This is the ambience that comes with this item'. What in fact we are buying is not so much the product as its sign value and the way in which it will differentiate us from others. Consumer products have come to "constitute a classification system that codes behaviour and groups."[42] So we have 'the Marlborough man', 'the Revlon look'.

Virtual reality has been developed to such a high degree that it can often prove more attractive and satisfying than the real world. For example, some simulation games provide you with a helmet and a cabin, and then place you in command of an ultra-modern aircraft locked in a combat duel with opposing 'enemy' fighters; or they set you in the cockpit of a Formula One racing car, competing against world-class drivers on a well-known racing track. Both experiences can cause you to pitch and roll as you manoeuvre. It is hard to convince yourself that in the end it is make-believe.

Yet all this is available without any fears of crashing, being shot down, having to answer to superiors for your actions, or walking away from a disaster with any sense of guilt. It is reality without responsibility. Why then involve yourself with all the risks inherent in the real thing when the virtual reality is just as exciting, but with total security?

This takeover of the real by the virtual, of the object by the image, is sometimes referred to as 'Disneyfying'. Some travellers return after weeks or months seeking to get close to the real Asia or the real America claiming that the highlight of their tour was the day they spent at Disneyland, the world of make-believe. Perhaps the most dramatic example of this trend in the postmodern world of communications was when television went live to show the world the landing of US peacekeeping troops in Somalia, with the conquering heroes stepping over TV cables and pausing to be interviewed by camera crews while they pursued their objective.

Information technology has also made possible 'virtual community' through a global network of those who are on the Internet, enabling a wide variety of people to discover one another quickly, communicate cheaply and participate in 'meetings'. But there is always the possibility these 'virtual communities' will not rise above the level of what Tony Hancock, the British radio comedian, once described in one of his comedy half-hours, *The Radio Ham*, as: "Great invention this radio. Gives me friends all over the world, all over the world, I say. None in this country, mind you. But all over the world."[43]

Such friendships are better than no friendships at all, but the capacity of modern society to magnify the possibilities for isolation as much as it creates facilities for understanding across distances has to be taken seriously.

If postmodernity in all its subtle variety and casualness has effectively undermined the confident steel and glass edifice of modernity, it has also brought with it a whole new set of challenges to the Church as much as it has to society, though both, it seems, are still too distracted by undealt items of business remaining from the agenda of modernity to be fully aware of this.

CHAPTER SIX

Culture Shifts
and the Christian Faith

Understanding modernity and postmodernity, and how each in turn has unsettled and reshaped Western societies, provides insight into the reason for much of the Christian malaise peculiar to the West today. The decline in the strength and position of the Christian Church in all Western nations over the last 50 years can be seen as a fall-out from these two major culture shifts of our time. But hopefully such understanding also begins to place us in a position to discern the way ahead for a reconstituted Christian Church as it embarks on the 21st century in a vastly changed world.

The Impact of Modernity on Western Theology

Modernity was constructed out of certain key Enlightenment principles. Over time these principles came to acquire the status of modern myths, determining the shape and substance of the world we have been living in for the past century or more. David Bosch[1] names seven of these marks of modernity that owe their origin to the Enlightenment, and that have evolved from these beginnings to form the paradigm of the Western world in the 20th century.[2] Each of them has also had some direct bearing on recent developments in Western theology. Over the last hundred years these theological perspectives have markedly affected the outlook and ethos of the Church in the West and, indirectly, of many Churches in the new world.

The first of these seven marks of modernity significantly affecting theology is the **primacy of reason**, what modernity considered the dominant facet of personhood in relationship to God. Under modernity, reason rather than faith became the measure of truth in knowing God. James D Hunter put it thus: "At the very least, the binding address of faith – the inner imperative binding people to inherited rules and guiding them in day-to-day details of their lives – has weakened. Belief has not dissolved, but the feeling of serene certainty has. Truth is no longer something unconsciously assumed but something to which one must consciously and intellectually assent."[3]

Several consequences followed from this:

- Theology was often kept separate from personal feelings and human experience. In two contrasting responses, faith then became located either in reason devoid of feeling (some liberal theology), or in experience dismissive of the intellect (some evangelical theology). An effective 21st century Christianity will require both contributions to be welcome ingredients of its theology. "Arguably, Christianity in the modern world needs the critical rationality of liberalism, because it is short on self-reflection. It certainly needs to harness religious enthusiasm, for the story needs to be told with verve and conviction if it is to be heard amidst the babble of our modern culture."[4]

- In some cases religion became privatised and unconnected to the public square: "Neither [Jesus nor Paul] would have recognised...the purely personal and private kind of religion which has now become common in the Western world. When Jesus preached about the coming of the Kingdom of God, he certainly did not mean just an internal spiritual experience for a few individuals."[5]

- Theology was claimed to constitute a science and then obliged to apply rationalistic principles to its study, and to justify its conclusions according to these same criteria. Some of the theological metanarratives that were developed under modernity, principally in the late 19th and early 20th centuries, and that imposed themselves like straitjackets on the theological colleges and university departments of theology up until the 1980s, were the concept of progressive revelation/education, the Wellhausen documentary theory, and more recently certain forms of liberation theology. Feminist theology has also been used as a metanarrative by which sense is made of the biblical records, and as a lens through which the whole history of the Christian Church is to be viewed.

- The end effect of such metanarratives is to create closed systems of theological study and interpretation at the expense, for example, of the rich diversity of the scriptural records, and in denial of the varied ways in which God can speak to different people and separate cultures through the Scriptures. One of the blessings brought by the postmodern reaction is a new freedom to allow the Scriptures or any other writings and experiences to speak for themselves. Where such a window of postmodernity has been opened in our departments of divinity, this has come as a breath of fresh air to the world of theological teaching. From late in the 19th century Anglicans were as ready as others to fall over themselves in order to bow at the altar of rationality, even its bishops meeting in conclave at Lambeth.[6]

Some Christians, in a 20th century adaptation of 17th century deism, embraced and affirmed secular society as the arena in which God was likely to be found at work, more than in the Church (for example, Bonhoeffer, Munby, Harvey Cox). "It may very well be that unbelief in society at large has more to do with the sociological process of secularization than with the philosophy of secularism, but this does not alter the fact that academic theology has drunk deep at the well of modern thought for over 200 years, and has only itself to blame for its present sickness."[7]

A second mark of modernity was the **subject-object distinction** observed by the natural sciences. This was also later applied to theology, especially in the field of biblical scholarship. This led variously to an immersion in hermeneutics on the part of some, or to an absorption in issues of scriptural inerrancy for others. Andrew Walker observes: "...that the work of many scholars in the modern era, as brilliant as much of it has been, has eclipsed the Gospel as narrative. Telling the story, the function of which is to reveal the Christ, has been replaced either by different gospels or by a critical re-evaluation of the grand narrative's constituent narrations. There has been a hermeneutical oppression whereby the story – now fragmented and disconnected – has had to await authentication from the critics in order to be told."[8]

A third way in which modernity has affected theology has been in its **elimination of purpose** as the proper explanation of all things, replacing this with a search for direct causality. In the minds of many modern Western Christians and church leaders human planning as a way of effecting a deter-mined outcome assumed greater significance than reliance upon God and a sense of Providence.

Too frequently modern ministers, of whatever denomination, came to see themselves more as managers than as shepherds, as CEOs rather than as pastors.

Fourthly, there was modernity's confident **belief in progress**. As a fundamental feature of the Age of Reason, this also captured the minds of Western theologians. The Christian faith came to be viewed as a vital element in the wider process of making the world a better place for all to live in, through the eradication of poverty and restoration of justice for all. Utopia was given its Christian version, to be achieved simply through appropriate legislative tinkering by politicians and planners, goaded and kept honest by the Church and its social prophets.

So God's kingdom became identified with the aspirations of the culture and civilization of the West. 'Development' was urged as the criterion by which to evaluate overseas missions, traditional or new. 'Intermediate technology' was the realistic goal, because Third World countries, it was assumed, had so much to catch up on, compared with the more developed countries of the West. The inference was that the First World had got it right: that was where everyone else needed to get to. The surprising thing is that this was still being urged by liberal-hearted Western Churches as recently as the 1970s, and that they were blind to the arrogance of such a posture!

The World Sets the Agenda

"Secularism's greatest success, however, is in the widespread demoral-
ization in the ranks of clergy and theologians who are supposed to
proclaim and interpret the truth of the Gospel but delude themselves
that they are achieving that purpose by adapting Christian faith and life
to the demands of secularism. What the situation requires...is precisely
the opposite of such uncritical adaptation."[9]

Wolfhart Pannenberg

Also having a far-reaching impact on Western theology was the paradig-
matic **fact-value distinctions** of the Enlightenment thinkers. First, Christian
faith was located in the realm of values. It then came to be seen as just one
value among many, all of more or less equal worth. Tolerance was called for
when addressing matters of subjective value rather than objective fact. In
the new climate created by modernity, tolerance became elevated into the
supreme Christian virtue above truth.

As many Christians themselves opted into this framework, the ancient
evangelical emphases of the Gospel lost their force. The prophetic role of
the Church to speak to others beyond its own membership, its missionary
mandate to reach into every land and nation, and confidence in its unique
doctrine and dogmas, were undermined. Lesslie Newbigin asserts that
Western Christians have grown timid, lost confidence in the Gospel and its
saving power, even forgotten the story of redemption, under the influence
of a century of liberal theologies shaped by the regime of rationality.[10]

Sixthly, a hallmark of the earliest Enlightenment thinkers from the
beginning was their confidence in the **solvability of all problems** and the
ability ultimately to explain all mysteries. In the late 19th century, this same
conviction steadily permeated the teaching of Western theology, leading to
a growing incredulity in Christian ranks towards miracles, rejection of the
inexplicable (e.g., the resurrection of Christ), and a dismissal of the
contradictory. This was triumphant liberalism of an enlightened European

civilization successfully and often without demur transposed into the Church.

Finally, another mark of the Enlightenment to infect Western theology was its focus on the **emancipated, autonomous individual**. At its heart and above all else, the Enlightenment was "a secular movement that sought the demystification and desacralization of knowledge and social organisation" (i.e., to take these out of the hands of the Church), "in order to liberate human beings from their chains. It took Alexander Pope's injunction:

> Know then thyself, presume not god to scan,
> The proper study of mankind is man,

with great seriousness."[11] In its worst expression this became the rampant individualism of both liberal and evangelical wings of Protestantism, and eventually the mobile, supermarket spiritual mentality of many contemporary Western Christians today.

Energetically shovelling both from the left and from the right, the institutional Church in the West in these ways helped dig its own grave as 'church' was allowed to become peripheral to faith, a place one chose to go to rather than a body one needed to belong to. And a choice of the moment that one might quite easily swap with another at a later time, as the fancy took one – just like shopping. In fact, the consumer became king, even in matters of faith.

Twentieth Century Reactions to Rampant Modernity

The advent of high modernity has not been universally well received. It has provoked, directly or indirectly, a number of reactions from within the Christian community. Other factors have also influenced the emergence of these responses. But without the wide success that modernity has had both in capturing the hearts and minds of the 20th century Western world, and in making an indelible impression on the rest of the world, it is debatable whether all or any of these religious reactions would have occurred.

First, there was the **rise of fundamentalism** from the late 1920s. This was not just a phenomenon of the Christian faith. It occurred in other major religions also, sometimes (as in Islamic fundamentalism and Jewish fund-amentalism) taking particular political and on occasions armed forms. Some Christian fundamentalist groups even took up arms, overtly or by storing up secret arsenals. It can be strongly argued that the rise of these fundamen-talist movements in quite different and unconnected regions and religions was more a cry of protest at the nature and degree of wider changes taking place in their societies through the forces of modernity (and at the threat to established ways and cherished values these changes seemed to pose) than the expression of a search for purity of faith and doctrine.

Secondly, there was the **rise of the charismatic movement** in Christian Churches around the world from the early 1960s. This almost exactly coincided with the progress of the advanced secular spirit and the advent of the 'God is dead' school of theology during that decade. The charismatic movement reached out particularly to those areas of life and faith neglected or disenfranchised by the modernist theologies of that time.

Such theologies and their impact had extended well beyond the academic debates and lecture theatres of theological colleges and departments of religious studies, and into the pews and parish councils of local churches. Aspects of faith called in question, or at times even ridiculed by the theological powerbrokers of that period, were belief in the miraculous, demonstrative expressions of feelings in worship, and recognition of personal spiritual gifts such as speaking in tongues. But above all, the straw that broke the camel's back was the refusal of the mainstream Churches of that time to do justice to teaching the presence and work of the Holy Spirit in the Church and in the individual believer. Many felt they were being left with a disembowelled Christianity.

A third reaction within the Church to high modernity was the emergence of a **resurgent evangelicalism**, dating from the late 1960s and evidenced in widely representative gatherings held about that time, such as the Keele National Assembly of Evangelical Anglicans in Great Britain during 1967 and the undenominational Lausanne International Congress of 1974. Three central themes dominated these gatherings and others like them over the following decade or more:

- a determination to remain within the denominational Churches, and win these back to a more biblical pattern of ministry and theology;

- rejection of the way liberal-dominated theological faculties had summarily dismissed Special Revelation and reduced the Scriptures to interesting historic writings containing mixtures of myth and memory; and

- espousal of a much more world-affirming, holistic understanding of God's mission and the Church's calling within that mission. This resurgence in evangelical Christianity continues unabated.

A particularly North American reaction to the impact of modernity on faith and theology has been the emergence there of **culturally captive Christianity**. This takes several different forms, all giving the appearance of being more greatly influenced in their formation by cultural than by theological factors. So, for example, over several decades in the U.S.A. there has been the development of professionally polished and (judging by their dollar-raising and vote-influencing achievements) highly effective *tele-vangelism*. The principle seems to be, when confronted with the slick and successful skills of media promotion as a mark of modernity in the secular sphere, "If you can't beat 'em, join 'em."

As modernity bites, so the status and prestige of other Christian ministry has suffered a reverse. In the United States some have responded to this diminishing profile by *majoring on management and therapy* as skills and emphases of ministry. Yet others have attempted to regain lost ground and restore diminished respect through *playing on the spectacular*, whether in infotainment-style worship transmitted by cable television, or by high-lighting the miraculous in contemporary terms through high profile healing ministries.

Still others have taken the idol of consumerism by the horns and developed a *health and prosperity gospel,* providing consumer-orientated Churches geared to well-researched client needs, accentuating only the positive, and kept before the public eye with promotional extravaganzas.

On the other hand, the Christian counterpart of rampant modernity, an all too often arrogant theological liberalism, has also experienced grievous

Malls and Megachurches

Malls and megachurches, each in their own way, are perfectly in tune with modernity. Both are monuments to consumption, and both celebrate the coupling of the appetites of consumption with religion.

The religion of the mall has been condensed into the secular creed that to have is to be; that of the megachurch (the hunger to consume) has been converted into the need to be spiritually nourished – but with the anonymity and freedom that allows one to be footloose, to pick and choose, to inspect at leisure, as in the shopping mall.

losses. Both modernity and liberalism were caught red-handed in the act of dismissal of the ancient, and charged with dependency on the rational. So the second half of the 20th century has witnessed a gradual demise of hard-line liberal theology with its astringent biblical criticism, in step with the decline of modernity.

A further change in the last quarter of the 20th century has been an evident recession of the ecumenical movement, both internationally and nationally. Ecumenical dreams of one Church for one world, and one Church for each nation, were wedded too closely to the universalist hopes of modernity. Such aspirations have not fitted well with the sea-change creeping into Western consciousness that increasingly is coming to emphasize diversity over uniformity, fragmentation over unity, the local over the universal, rejection of all grand dreams and accounts of the world in favour of a multi-tude of little stories, and pessimism concerning the world rather than bright-eyed optimism. The late 20th century dissection of modernity has been accompanied by a dissipation of institutional ecumenism as the blueprint for the future. Both have risen and fallen together.

On the credit side, thankfully, this has not introduced a new era of hostility or even suspicion between the major Christian Churches. Adapting to the different drum beat of an increasingly postmodern consciousness, much 'functional' (as opposed to 'institutional') ecumenism is taking place

– but not at the expense of having to barter away the distinctives of any Church. Rather, it is an open faced ecumenism that trusts more, works together better, responds more quickly in more ad hoc ways, all without the necessity of legal agreements and formulas, interminable committees and consultations, and the need to devise a theology to go with it.

Modernity's Success in Undoing the Past

One cannot doubt the honourable intentions of the fathers of the Enlightenment or the sincerity of the architects of modernity. Both had the welfare of humanity in mind in their projects, and both believed it was first necessary to liberate humanity from the shackles and constrictions of the past that were impeding the advance of civilization. Neither could see that in dismantling the scaffolding of an earlier society they were reducing the capacity of Western communities to withstand the very winds of change that they were anticipating.

The success of modernity in dismantling vestigial structures of the pre-modern world can be measured in a number of different ways:

First, there was its success in disempowering hierarchies of power and class in society. In the eyes of many this task is still not yet complete. Certainly there were (and still are) injustices and inequities in the ordering of society. Some always seem to do better than others, and too often on the grounds of birth and privilege rather than because of merit or effort. The good things of this life are not always distributed fairly.

But the positive achievements in this area cannot be exaggerated, particularly the increasing emancipation of women in a male-dominated society. Breaking class barriers and social stigmas also opened doors of opportunity in education and advancement to many who formerly had been under life sentence to 'keep their place'.

Yet with all its shortcomings, and whether for good or ill, stratified society provided a security of identity for some alongside the inequalities of such a system. In destroying these hierarchies, modernity has also unintentionally induced a loss of belonging in many others, a disquieting sense of anomie. And for them this has been a heavy price to pay.

Immanuel Kant

Immanuel Kant (1724-1804), son of committed Lutheran parents and a firm Christian believer himself, writing in the early 19th century and looking back at the successes of the Enlightenment in emancipating Europe from the stultifying atmosphere of premodern times, could speak of: "The emergence of human beings from a tutelage to which they had voluntarily acceded...Tutelage is the inability to make use of one's own understanding without being guided by another. 'Dare to know', have the courage to make use of your own understanding! That is the slogan of the Enlightenment."[12]

Second, there has been modernity's success in undermining ancient institutions and respect for the distant past. Certainly both in the beginning, at the time of the Enlightenment, and still later, at the threshold of late modernity, there were some long-standing institutions of society that were well overdue for reform, yet refused to countenance change. Even as late as 1997, in the emotion and debate arising out of the tragic death of the Princess of Wales, one of the deep concerns that surfaced was public perception of the way the Royal Family inadequately related to modern times and values. The widespread sense of anguish at the death of Princess Diana seemed to be as much an unbearable grief over the loss of a royal personage who at last appeared to reflect the mood and manner of the times, as it was inconsolable sorrow over the premature death of a young mother so beautiful, caring, popular and at the prime of life.

But in attacking these institutions from the past because they belonged to another era, and discrediting them in the eyes of the public, the message was often being conveyed that all that was old was out – *passé*, that everything needed to change, that age and venerability were negative values, not positive.

We are now reaping the consequences of this in a widespread (yet thankfully not universal) disregard for the ancient and the yesteryear. Modernity has contributed to this loss of interest in history, this discomfort with the process of ageing and lack of appreciation that the era of technology does not have a corner on wisdom. Once respect for the past and its institutions begins to die, some also begin to question all the symbols and bearers of authority within society of that day.

"Do not forsake me now that I am old and grey headed:
till I have made known the strength of your arm
to the generations that are yet to come."

Psalm 71: 18, *A New Zealand Prayer Book*

Third, as another mark of the success of the Enlightenment's and (later) modernity's impact on theology, there is the legacy of the removal of any reliance on revelation as a primary source of spiritual understanding for determining matters of belief or behaviour. By moving God to the margins of life, by making religious faith a private matter, by elevating reason to Chief Judge of the Court of Appeal, the role of revelation in unveiling truth has sometimes been reduced to a point of insignificance. But this also means that there is no final bar to appeal to other than the bar of one's own reason, no God to seek or to listen to other than the still small voice within – and too often that voice conveniently seems to say the kind of things we want it to say.

Fourth, as another achievement of modernity in undoing the structures and values of the past there was the dispensing with any remaining inbuilt sense of sin, guilt or accountability to God for one's life and actions. Modernity seeping in to the Church began by making these older attitudes and beliefs look foolish. There was talk of Cranmer, principal compiler of the old Anglican Prayer Book, requiring us to 'grovel in sin'. Some traditional church services and practices were accused of setting out to induce feelings of guilt for the benefit of exercising the priestly powers of forgiveness. The Day of Judgement was reduced to an end time when all social injustices would be corrected.

Then two decades of reflective and non-value-laden counselling by cohorts of clergy led to no one feeling anything they did was ever wrong. These clericalized counsellors in high places often joined the mood of modernity in ridiculing any sense of there actually being 'right' or 'wrong'. Evil was construed as largely institutional, the prerogative of the big corporations – never something that could be laid at the feet of the ordinary person. Personal responsibility for one's actions was often replaced by an attachment of blame to 'societal factors'.

Fifth, the Church through its embracing of modernity cannot be held solely responsible for the dismissal of religion as the social cement of public life, and the rejection of God as the One who gives each and all of us our true personal identity. On the contrary, church leaders in the post-World War II period often strove valiantly to re-establish the central role of the Church in society and public life. But to no avail.

It was a battle they could not win, because it was no longer the kind of society that saw any need for God in its public life, or in a search for personal identity. Secularization, as the religious face of modernity, was by now too strongly entrenched in societies such as New Zealand. (In Great Britain two exceptional factors delayed by decades this effect – the Church of England had an established place and role in society by law and tradition, and overwhelming reminders of a Christian past were to be seen on every hand in the nation's life.)

Moreover, aided and abetted by many within the Church, the endless search of modern men and women for self-meaning and identity was diverted to the counselling couches and therapy centres of the new industry of psychoanalysis, rather than pointed towards God.

Where once the Christian Church was the most respected institution of society in the Western world, modernity saw to it that along with other institutions that belonged to a past age and another way of thinking, **the Church was not only given a low profile but also periodically made to look a buffoon.** In countries like New Zealand, this was driven home by some sections of the media. News of the Churches' activities, exposure to a specifically Christian voice and viewpoint, and public access to prominent church leaders were kept to a minimum. Television programmes such as *All*

Gas and Gaiters made clergy look morons and the Church look foolish. Vicars, until the mid-1990s, were invariably made to appear as dim-witted, out of touch, and not at all in the same image as scientists, artists, doctors or lawyers. Thankfully this has begun to change, but perhaps as much due to the new winds of postmodernity as to any sense of fairness or respect on the part of TV producers and programmers.[13]

However, provide a clerical scandal, or a political *faux pas* on the part of a church leader, and some sections of the media will be quick to make the shame and anguish as public as possible. Perhaps it could be construed as a back-handed tribute to a lingering high regard for church leaders that in Great Britain the misfortunes of Roman Catholic Bishop Roddy Wright in September 1996, caught up in a relationship with one of his parishioners, could have evoked such a high-profile media response.

Modernity has also been largely responsible for **the elimination of any recognition of humankind's need of a saviour** – beyond what one can hopefully achieve through one's own powers and resources. The pinnacle of modernity's achievements was not only to place men on the moon or to reconstruct the nature of plants and crops through genetic engineering. It was also to remove any generally held conviction that in these modern times anyone needs a saviour. All the answers any of us would ever need lie to hand without recourse to God.

Here again, some support for such a viewpoint was at times provided by certain theologians and Christian teachers who questioned whether Christianity really had anything more to offer than other similar religions. Often these same people also questioned the concept of atonement, any talk of Jesus Christ dying for the sin of the world, and biblical ideas of sacrifice and offering. In 1996, during a radio interview in New Zealand on the National Programme, a minister, previously on the staff of a theological college, expressed the view that "Christians may not have a monopoly on God...Jesus was quite aware that he had a special vocation...and the Church defined Jesus as being divine. We name Jesus in our own setting...but how that happens for people in other settings is a question for them...God is the impulse at work [and we have] the revealing of this in powerful religious personages such as Jesus." His lay associate in this interview was no less adamant: "How can you have the arrogance to say that the God Christians worship is the true God, and all others are false?"

Strangely, no opportunity for a different way of presenting an understanding of the person of Jesus Christ was provided by the producer of that programme. It makes modernity's protestations about balance and fairness run thin. Later that same year a senior religious studies lecturer and accredited minister, speaking of Jesus Christ in a public lecture in New Zealand, said: "As a historical figure he was not divine but created to be divine by the Church."[14] It all sounded like further contributions to modernity's great demolition job, but this time with the aid of white ants from within.

Such a riveted attention to this world and the immediate personal needs of humanity now, along with a hermeneutic of suspicion concerning God, a world beyond, and the unseen realm of angels and archangels – all served to **extract from modern life any sense of mystery, wonder, and awe**, any awareness of the numinous. This too became a further entry on the debit side of modernity that one day a new generation would call to account.

Along with this went **the loss of a sense of the sacred in the public arena** – buildings, persons, moral principles, ancient ways, all became prized primarily in terms of their intrinsic architectural beauty or their utilitarian value, and then only in the eyes of the beholder. When God counts for little, symbols of the spiritual, buildings for worship, memorials to the heroes of the past – they too begin to lose their aura.

And we are all diminished by this, quite beyond the damage vandals do to the material structures. Modernity, in its shifting of perspectives and values, must take much of the responsibility for this.

Sixth, there was the damage done to the corporate nature of belief and of the walk of faith. All share responsibility for this in some measure, the Church no less than society at large. By the elevation of 'the autonomous self' to the pinnacle of life (through promotion of individual rights legislation and action, for example), in societies now assumed to be secular, modernity made its contribution to the downsizing of 'community' in the new world it was recreating.

Christians have been largely blind to what has been happening behind the scenes in societies that have wholeheartedly embraced the principles of the Enlightenment. The Christian Church is caught up in the rush of the Gadarene swine along with everyone else. We have done this by our insistence on the importance of individual salvation, personal responses of faith, private prayer times, 'Jesus and me' spirituality and hymnody, and how each one of us must stand on our own before the throne of God at the Judgement Day and answer for her or his own self. We have reinforced this sense of a faith where belief belongs entirely to the individual, and this sense of a discipleship that is solely a personal journey which need not be walked through or worked out in the company of others.

Shaped by Modernity, Disturbed by Postmodernity

We are coming to realise that we find ourselves today in Churches that have been largely shaped by modernity – in outlook if not in structure. But they are also Churches feeling the cold winds of change as the fresh challenges of postmodernity disturb their comfortable accommodation with the Enlightenment project. As we enter the 21st century such challenges brought by the mood of postmodernity are likely to be in these areas:

- **Valuing the local and the particular, over against modernity's vision of the universal**. As we move through the early decades of the 21st century, significance is more likely to lie with a rural congregation meeting in the back reaches of a remote New Zealand valley, or with Polynesians in a metropolitan city recapturing something of their own culture and colour in a Sunday afternoon service at a time when they can have a local suburban church to themselves – rather than with grand talk about a world-wide Church, and denominations that span the globe.

- **Diversity applauded, rather than the modernist penchant for uniformity and conformity**. There is no universally valid, ideal design for every international airport terminal, or way an up-market business manager in any capital city should dress, or stereotyped style of being a Western Christian. A prevailing postmodern attitude to life is likely to say: "Let each place and each person work out what is appropriate and what feels best for them." Churches will increasingly have to discover how to accommodate this diversity, with all its risks and untidiness, within their inherited structures and traditional liturgies.

This means delighting in difference, rather than encouraging a narrow band of sameness. Why should this year's fashion magnates dictate what we wear? Why need our outfit be always colour coordinated and material matching? The indications are that postmodernists will go for eclecticism and contrast, a little piece from the 1960s, a touch of Tudor England, some leather, a Pakistani cap, and lace-up boots. What matters is how we feel and the impression we create. And what applies to clothes under the influence of postmodernity, in another generation could be how a postmodern generation approaches faith and worship.

- **Plurality seen as appreciating many truths, rather than as tolerance of different views.** Under modernity, pluralism meant not allowing any person or any group to assert exclusive claims to truth at the expense of others, for truth was seen to be larger than any single expression of it. So, for example, a modernist explanation would say that all religions contain some insights into the ultimately true, so all need to be valued as different ways pointing to this greater truth. But there was a final truth – it was only the approaches to it that varied.

Under postmodernity however, pluralism means something different. Now it means recognizing and accepting the stories of all peoples, not as windows into some greater truth, for there is no such thing, but as contrasting yet authentic ways in which peoples variously express their values and account for their identity. Each religion, even each interest group within a society, is to be given status and space simply for its own sake. So postmodernity contributes to a fragmentation of the social body into numerous segments as well as faiths, e.g., the 'greens', 'lesbian/gays', 'feminists', etc., each having an agenda and a place in the sun of their own.

The increasingly pluralistic scene in Western societies, dating back to the high days of modernity, challenges the uniqueness of Christ alongside other religious leaders, and the truthfulness of the Christian message as against the teaching of other faiths. Modernity had asked simply for *tolerance of others' views*. Postmodernity, however, shifts the ground and sees pluralism as the *abandonment of any public truth* so that all that remains is what any group chooses as truth for them. David Lyon makes the observation: "Whereas tolerance was once believed to be founded in unique truth, the irony is that pluralism – which that tolerance permitted – now requires that truth be abandoned."[15]

In the end, the greatest challenge pluralism may present in this new century could be not so much to the Christian Church as to the structure-less world that postmodernity is inheriting. The acceptance of plurality may lead to the presence of so many options of life, together with the absence of certainty about any one of them in particular, that the human frame cannot bear the load. Peter Berger courageously interprets such challenges with a positive optimism: "As pluralism undermines the certainties of religious absolutism, it also weakens any secular forms of dogmatism...Pluralism makes any quest for certainty more difficult: it encourages scepticism rather than faith, cognitive and normative open-ness rather than closure. But human beings have a deeply rooted urge for certainty and faith, and the endless openness of pluralism – especially in moral matters – is difficult to bear."[16] This could well prove, then, not so much a threat to the Christian faith as a window of opportunity through which the Church is potentially well equipped to respond.[17]

- **Surface signs of postmodernity challenging the modernist search for deeper meaning**. Postmodernity brings a note of playfulness and mock irony to the scene. Should all of life be so serious? Why should not Cheeta the chimpanzee join Peter Blake in presenting a high profile exhib-ition at the National Gallery in London? Must reality always be hidden beneath the surface and have to be quarried to be enjoyed? 'Let signs and symbols be a language of the moment, a discourse of the surface, enjoyed for their own sake', is one message of postmodernity for the world of the 21st century. This will have consequences for the Church in its presentation of the Word made flesh. 'Bookish' worship is likely more and more to yield ground to the visual and the sensory, well-orchestrated rituals to warm relationships, learned sermons to memorable symbols.

- **Feeling good matters more than modernity's emphasis on thinking correctly**. Postmodernity suggests a tiring in Western societies induced by the relentless litanies of political correctness, with all their assumptions about the central significance of the sole person in his or her individual rights. What *feels* right, taking into consideration *the good of the whole*, is more important to the postmodernist than involved arguments and appeals to this or that supposed insensitivity in order to crank up personal rights a notch or two.

  Postmodernity may well move society from intricate political debates, with their environment of litigiousness, towards a common consensus based on intuition and feeling. In New Zealand midway through the 1990s, the arguments for a change in the system of parliamentary election, expressed in the move to an MMP-style of proportional representation, seemed to reflect such a popular hope that the constituency had been trying to convey to the politicians. This also the Church will need to take into account in the way issues are debated and just causes pursued.

- **Visual image seen to be more important than the printed word**. It is more than just television that is gradually conditioning our world to receive its messages through images. Images abound even where TV is not watched. Signals are sent out by our choices of clothing; advertising hoardings on roadsides are becoming art forms; promotional materials with catchy brand logos fill our letter boxes; the packaging and presentation of goods at the Supermarket are designed to catch our eye.

  The printed word has not disappeared – nor will it ever be lost – but it now serves more and more as an interpretation of a message primarily and powerfully conveyed and received through image. What does this say, then, as to how Christians communicate: preachers, teachers, worship leaders, youth leaders, parish magazine editors, publicists, parents?

- **Life is sensed by the postmodern to be fleeting rather than fixed**. It is to be entered into now, rather than planned for the future. Looking back and savouring a past that is irrelevant, or looking forward and preparing

Neo-paganism

"The critical movement intended to clear the ground of beliefs and superstitions inherited from the past so that it could create a structure of indubitable truth; instead, the movement has ended by creating a vacant site into which new follies and superstitions are crowding. Could the leaders of the Age of Reason have ever imagined that, two centuries after their work, the forces of astrology, witchcraft, and black magic would once again capture hearts and minds in a Europe that enjoyed... that universal education which was one of their dreams?"[18]

for a future that is uncertain, has less meaning for those who are constantly being conditioned, albeit unconsciously, by the outlook of postmodernity. So the symbol of this new generation is more likely to be the credit card than the savings book. "I have come that you may have life, and have it more abundantly" is likely to be the theme that sits better with the 21st century postmodern than "I go to prepare a place for you, that where I am there you may be also."

• **The hesitancy of the postmodern mind, compared with the assurance of the modern.** Even the Church, under the influence of modernity, at times has displayed a touch of arrogance in the way it has commended its message. Such confidence, those evangelists and great preachers of the post-war period showed. They had the answers. They were as confident about their position as the secondary school biology teacher was about 'the assured findings of science'. And they let it be known. But the postmodern scientist and the postmodern church leader, even if they are right, both know that they need to be more humble in their protestations and more restrained in their proclamations, treating those who listen as equal, not equine, as they meet up with the hearts and minds of a new generation.

• Appreciation of the spiritual as a real dimension of human awareness.

Postmodernity's Challenge to the Church

"Western culture is in the middle of a fundamental transformation: a 'shape of life' is growing old. The demise of the old is being hastened by the end of colonialism, the uprising of women, the revolt of other cultures against white Western hegemony, shifts in the balance of economic and political power within the world economy, and a growing awareness of the costs as well as the benefits of scientific and technological 'progress'.

As we approach the end of the 20th century, modernity is in radical decline. Its legitimating myths are no longer believed with any conviction. The old 'sacred canopy' of modern progress which had previously sheltered the inhabitants of modernity has blown off the fourth floor and the biting chill of anomie now settles on the 'naked public square'. The result is that we are exposed to radical insecurity and to...the gravest sort of anxiety...It is not as though people fear clearly defined threats. Rather it feels as if our whole culture has the willies. Intelligent, high-powered, well-educated people are worried about making what used to be ordinary life decisions like entering into committed relationships and having children.

Culturally, everything seems to be falling apart. Beliefs that were once certain and widely held – like...the ability to solve all environmental problems by more Western technological ingenuity, the strength and durability of the capitalist market system, and the superiority of the Western intellectual tradition – are all being questioned on a daily basis...

If God doesn't wake us up to this postmodern tragedy, one day we are going to have the sort of rude awakening the builders and dreamers of the Tower of Babel got when, just as they thought they had accomplished their purpose and reached as high as heaven, God scattered and dispersed them in judgement. It is time for Christians to realize that we are living in a culture that is reaping the bitter fruits of its own distorted ideals."[19]

This is already a mark of the postmodern mentality. Compare this with the ever-ready dismissal of the supernatural by the more earthbound modernists. Yet, rather than the eventual rejection of all religion at the turn of the century, as had been confidently predicted by the secular theologians of the 1960s at the height of modernity,[20] the last two decades of the 20th century witnessed an unexpected resurgence of neo-paganism in the Western world, and a wide acceptance of the occult. So at the very time when technology and psychotherapy had reached dizzy heights of achievement, we also saw an unexpected growth of astrology and various forms of spiritual healing. Not less religiosity then, with the infiltration of technological society by postmodernity, but new, different and often incredibly irrational expressions of it.

The task we face as Churches entering the 21st century is daunting, but the prospects under God are also pregnant with hope – if we can but read our world aright, discern the purposes of God afresh, and act accordingly.

CHAPTER SEVEN

Rethinking the Church
for a New Century

As the Western world moves into the 21st century, working out what it means to be a Church within an increasingly postmodern climate has significant implications for Christian mission and ministry. This is true of every Church, but even more true of older, mainline Churches, with their rich accumulation of tradition drawn initially from a premodern past, and their highly developed structures and pastoral systems shaped and given a particular mind-set under modernity. If these traditional Churches are perceived to have the problem of identifying too closely with an older world and another age, the problem of the newer Churches is likely to be that of too closely identifying with the subtle values and outlook of this present world and this current age.

Rethinking the Church's Ministry

The difficulties begin with the growing realization that both the more traditional Churches and the newer independent Churches have ministries that may be as much culturally conditioned as Gospel-driven. The former for the most part have been designed and their ministry ordered for a subtly different society and significantly different task.

The challenge to these older Churches is to rethink the style and priorities of the ordained ministry they offer in what has now become a largely changed world.

In the course of the 20th century certain changes to traditional styles of ministry were already taking place – but more as a response to the changing climate of late modernity rather than as preparation for the emerging era of postmodernity. Robert Bellah observes that two of the contemporary models of ministry were shaped by the essential interests of 20th century Western culture: ministries in the style of the psychologist and the manager. Both types are this-worldly, centred on the autonomous individual, driven by pragmatic rather than ideological interests, and both are hostile to the old moral order. In fact there are many points of similarity between them. Both seek to define life by the control they exercise over it, the one with respect to the inner world and the other with respect to the outer world.[1]

Certain assumptions therefore, formed in a different social climate, whether recent or ancient, lie behind the way most Churches see their calling. There is for some the assumption of **a still existing Christendom** justifying, for example in the Anglican Church, the traditional operational units of 'parish' and 'diocese'. These describe the Church territorially, in terms of tracts of land defined by their external boundaries, rather than spiritually, in terms of worship centres and faith communities bringing together those committed to Jesus Christ in any given area. The territorial models of organization were a direct adaptation of Roman Imperial divisions of civil government. These made sense even within a disintegrating empire that, following the conversion of Constantine, continued to own the Christian faith as the official religion everywhere within its borders. Every acre of the empire was in this way considered to be the pastoral responsibility of some priest and within some parish.

But 1500 years later, and after the battering received in recent times from secularization (the religious expression of the modern project), we ask whether the traditional parish system is still in every situation the most appropriate way of ordering the ministry and life of a contemporary Church? There has been a steadily increasing awareness of the inadequacies of the parish concept as the answer to all situations of church mission and ministry.

Christendom

The Church we know so well was a Church shaped for another era, and that era was Christendom. Christendom refers to the time when Europe publicly acknowledged Christ as Lord. Kings ruled by divine right; justice was based on the Ten Commandments and the teachings of Christ; oaths were sworn on the Bible; archbishops and bishops ranked in status close to royalty; the power of the Pope was a balance to the power of any Emperor; there was a church at the heart of every village; the priest or parson was the local seat of wisdom; schools and hospitals came into existence under the patronage of the Church; university colleges were identified by their unashamedly Christian affiliations. People still are proud to be a Fellow of Trinity or St John's in Cambridge, or of Christ's or Magdalene at Oxford. Students enrolled with Jesus College, Emmanuel or Corpus Christi. It was a world which assumed at the heart of its learning an overarching presence of God, the central place of the Church and the truth of the Christian faith.

For example, Andrew Walker writes: "Sociologically...the Churches have not declined because of apostasy...They have broken down because of the increasing irrelevancy of the parish system. Sadly, but true nevertheless, parishes are rarely natural communities any more – they are no longer viable plausibility structures. Local territory is not synonymous with homogeneity. In the inner cities, parishes rarely operate as natural localities."[2]

Church structures have not always been of this nature, as though this had always been of the essence of a Church that was to be true to the Apostles and their teaching. Before the reluctant Augustine and his mission landed in Kent in 597, the already existing Celtic model of ministry in Britain had been based on local communities of faith, sometimes expressed in monasteries under the leadership of an abbot (but with a bishop as part of the monastic community), sometimes in neighbourhood clusters of congregations accountable to a bishop in their midst. Might this suggest a structure more suited to our own times, at least for many situations?

Christendom implies a further assumption of that wider neighbourhood being one in which **most inhabitants will have been baptized**, or at very least where they will acknowledge a basic faith in God, and understand the essentials of the Christian story. So ministry with such an assumption is weighted towards pastoral care, and extended to all within any given area without discrimination. Mission in these circumstances is seen more as reminding people of the faith they are already presumed to have – even if it is dormant – than as calling people out of unbelief to faith in Jesus Christ.

The Anglican Church, for example, was both shaped for and by this kind of society. It was a Church designed for another world and with a particular role to play in that world. This was a pastoral model of life and ministry, with structures and expectations that reflected this. Over the last hundred years, though the world about it was changing with increasing rapidity, the Church has clung doughtily to the institutions and structures coming out of that Christendom past. In some urban areas today there are still 'rural deans'! This pastoral model remains deeply embedded in our character, creating in many places confusing expectations of the Church and its clergy by its lay members, and what 'ministry' will reliably deliver to them.

Also there continues today to be an assumption of **a clear theological differentiation between the ordained and the lay people of God**, to the extent of sustaining in some parts of the Church a latter-day clericalism at a time when other authority structures and hierarchies of power in society are being flattened. Under postmodernity there may well be a need for the Church to revisit its theology of clerical and lay members of the Church, in the light not only of what had been initially developed as appropriate for the era of Christendom, but also for what is now theologically appropriate for these current times, when 'Christendom' is no longer a reality.

In fact, surprising similarities can be discerned between the Church's position in the world of the 1st century and the climate in which that early Christian Church had to minister and carry out its mission, and the position of Christians in many parts of the West at the end of the 20th century and the environment of disdain within which the Church finds itself today.

A Different Mind-set?

In the world of the 21st century, a world that has been first of all refashioned by modernity then critiqued by postmodernity, there are new ways of seeing, knowing and communicating which any Christian Church will have to take into account if it is to make effective contact with this increasingly different generation – for example:

- Emphasising the local alongside the universal, the many stories alongside the one story, in a way that the Church has not needed to do for centuries.
- Starting at rock bottom, 'telling the story' afresh, God's story, as a way of commending the Christian message, rather than assuming that the world really must know all this already, and might find such an approach too simple. Lesslie Newbigin, describing the importance of 'story' to the Christian tradition, has written: "...wherever we turn we find the require-ment that we must believe in order to know. And knowing is an activity we engage in rather than something that happens to us. It only takes place as we seek to achieve. Hence the biblical story is most often in the form of narrative rather than concepts and propositions; i.e., God doing something and calling us to be involved, rather than God explaining something and asking us to understand. It is the uniqueness of this narrative, the story the Bible tells and which reaches its quintessence in the coming of Jesus, which has made Europe as a distinct cultural entity. It is impossible to understand the distinctive nature of European culture without grasping the special shaping role of this story."
- Shifting from a gospel of the individual, with the need for a purely private and personal response, to a gospel that is to be accepted, believed and lived out in a community of faith.
- Commending an holistic gospel that embraces the whole of human concerns (including physical, social, sexual, and environmental issues of humanity today), rather than a narrowly spiritual gospel concerned only with an individual's relationship to God.

God as Other

"...without a vision of God as Other, different from and standing over against the modern world, there is no compelling reason to think thoughts about the world that are not essentially modern.

It is this holiness of God then...that provides the light that exposes modernity's darkness for what it is. For modernity has emptied life of serious moral purpose. Indeed, it empties people of the capacity to see the world in moral terms, and this in turn closes their access to reality, for reality is fundamentally moral...[This is] why sin and grace have become such empty terms...Divorced from the holiness of God, sin is merely self-defeating behaviour or a breach in etiquette. Divorced from the holiness of God, grace is merely empty rhetoric, pious window dressing...Divorced from the holiness of God, our Gospel becomes indistinguishable from any of a host of alternative self-help doctrines. Divorced from the holiness of God, our public morality is reduced to little more than an accumulation of trade-offs between competing private interests. Divorced from the holiness of God, our worship becomes mere entertainment."[3]

David Wells

- Conveying a strong sense of 'the holy' by unveiling both the reality of God and the glory of God in a world now much more open to the spiritual, yet unable to give it a name.

- Acknowledging responsibility for our planet along with (even before!) hope of heaven. There is a strong British Christian tradition, traceable back to Celtic beginnings, that sees redemption as embracing the whole created order, the heavens and the earth and all creation united in praise to God. But this is also 'holistic' in the sense of spurning that particular innovation of modernity that separates the public realm from the private, facts from values, what we believe to be true from what we know to be true. This was never the way of pre-industrial societies, or of the ancient

Celtic Church to which the Anglican and Presbyterian denominations particularly owe more in their distinctive ethos and worldview than has been adequately acknowledged.

• Contributing a distinct realism about the world and its future, contrasted with either the discredited optimism of modernity or the prospectless pessimism of postmodernity. Theological Hall Principal Graham Cray comments: "Progress has turned out to be just another ideology with a limited shelf life...The initial impact of Enlightenment thinking was to create a society with a sense of liberation from the past and a shared vision of modern history as a movement with a direction. The collapse of the ideological assumption of progress has resulted in a loss of confidence in a significant future. Social coherence depends strongly on a sense of shared history and shared hope for the future. We only know who we are if we have a notion of how we have become and of where we are going."[4]

This Is Also Likely to Mean Rethinking...

Our way of reading the Scriptures

It will require of 21st century believers more constant reading, while at the same time a more intentional search for the larger story and not just 'a daily message in a verse'. In this way a new generation of Christians may learn to 'indwell' the Scriptures, and be shaped in faith and discipleship through them.

Hearing the public reading of a couple of short passages of the Bible in church on Sundays, or relying on the knowledge we picked up in scripture lessons at school in decades past, or even a few rushed verses a day as a personal spiritual discipline, may not get us through as Christians living in the aftermath of modernity. Once again, we need to become a people more soaked in the Word of God than we are conditioned by the spin doctors of the secular media whose words and images we find ourselves encountering at every point of work and domestic life.

Even for Christian families, this has become a real concern. "Christian parents know that the chances of socializing their children into the faith are slim, because as soon as they set foot outside their front door, they are entering a pluralistic world of a thousand siren voices. And when they are locked up indoors, watching television in their rooms, they hear the same voices, but this time in stereo and accompanied by seductive imagery."[5]

Our evangelism

The 1950s were a far more 'God-friendly' and 'Gospel-aware' age than the times we live in now. "The typical *non*believer of the 1950s more than likely had the following in their spiritual résumé: a belief in the deity of Christ; a conviction that truth existed and that the Bible was trustworthy; a positive image of the Church and its leaders; a church background, knowledge and experience that was relatively healthy; and a built-in sense of guilt or shame whenever they violated the basic values of the Judeo-Christian heritage, even if they declared themselves agnostics and never went near a church. This is why many of the evangelistic approaches of the 1950s *worked* in the 1950s."[6]

But today 'evangelism' translates "Don't tell me – show me." The Gospel will be more credible, winsome, and understood where it is seen to be affecting markedly the lives of ordinary people who we all know. Crucial to this will be a 'good news' quality of worship, friendship, and practical identification with the surrounding community found in each local church across the land, whatever the denomination.

"If we cannot demonstrate the proof of our story by living it, we will never convince people of its truth by talking about it."

Andrew Walker

Postmodernity is a condition where people want to see and experience rather than be told and exhorted. The most effective evangelism will be letting the Gospel speak through who we are and how we live, just as the first believers through the quality of their corporate and individual lives attracted the communities around them to look seriously at the person of Jesus and the message of the Gospel.[7]

As it was said many centuries ago: "Proclaim the Gospel by every means – if necessary, use even words." At some point those disillusioned by the times they live in, and drawn to another way of living exemplified in a Gospel community, will ask the question first put to the Apostles Peter and John after Pentecost: "By what power or in what name have such as you done this?"

Our church programmes

In this new century greater prominence will need to be given to discipleship courses and Christian formation. Firstly, because those who come to believe will require help in translating faith into everyday living – into their citizenship responsibilities, into discovering what it means to build a Christian society, into family and marriage relationships, singleness and social graces. For centuries previously a person born in the West could practically assume that Christian faith was a common possession of their civilization, that Christian virtues would naturally rub off on to them through socialization in the context of a community that corporately held to Christian beliefs and values, that their political and civic leaders would be guiding the nation or their city from the basis of Christian principles.

This can no longer be assumed. Since the 1980s there has been a growing grass roots recognition of the need to be much more intentional in Christian discipleship. Fewer people today become Christians by osmosis (catching the faith from home and community without being aware of it). There are likely to be increasing points of difference of view and of values. One option – or temptation – for Christians is to capitulate to the spirit of the age that motivates many of our politicians and professional leaders and accept whatever is going without demur. The other option is to attend with diligence to these matters and thus make their own distinctive contribution to the reshaping of their societies. If the latter is the course those who have come freshly to faith in Christ are to follow, then discipleship programmes will be needed to assist them. New Christians will look to their Churches for this help.

But secondly, there will also need to be a greater emphasis on discipleship training, because those coming to faith will be coming from a much further way off. More and more people are situated further and further away from the Gospel story. The distance to travel between unbelief and belief is much greater today than at any time for the past one thousand years. It will not be enough to have a cup of tea at the manse, parsonage, or vicarage and one or two talks with the minister once a commitment to follow the way of Christ has been made.

There is so much they will want to learn, so much they do not yet know, so much of their lives and values they will want to review. Opportunity for this will need to be provided in every Church expecting to survive beyond its current generation.

So far as the Anglican world is concerned, around the globe there has been mounting awareness of this through the phenomenal development of a range of both home grown and imported courses in making disciples, covering both how to introduce people to Jesus Christ and his Church, and then how to socialize them into this faith – courses such as Basic Christianity, Enquirers' Groups, Christian Beginnings, house group ministry, and, more recently, highly developed new routes to faith such as the Alpha programme.[8] But also some parts of the Church have revived ancient paths to faith and life within a worshipping community, such as the catechumenate.

Our way of looking at life
We will need to learn how to evaluate all things through Gospel lenses. This is an acquired skill that Christians old and new will have to discover afresh through good teaching.

The New Testament Epistle writers saw this as an important task in their generation. The content of the apostolic Letters to the Churches reveal the priority they gave to this. Very often the second half of each Epistle they wrote provided practical applications to everyday life in the first century of Gospel principles they had spelled out in the first half.

Furthermore, in the teaching of the Apostles, little of this was presented by way of vague generalities or pious clichés – they described without apology the world as it was, sometimes in all its grubbiness, and prescribed Christian conduct in detail as they saw it in that kind of world. We in our day will need to develop a new generation of lay and ordained ministers who are gifted teachers of the faith and skilled communicators of the word in the same mould.

Our way of praying

The place of prayer in the changed environment of the postmodern world may also need to be reconsidered. That could mean recovering the neglected art of 'practising the presence of God', as a 21st century application of an ancient spirituality – learning to pray as we drive to work, as we walk the children to school, as we watch people pass by while pausing at traffic lights, offering instant praise or thanksgiving to God at any moment of gratitude in our lives, bowing our heads without embarrassment to say a brief grace in a restaurant, invoking the Holy Spirit to guide and govern as we make a decision or meet a client.[9] It is reaching right back in our roots to recapture that older, Celtic attitude to prayer as living constantly with God as One who is interested in all the daily duties and mundane chores of our ordinary lives.

Our example of community

One of the most powerful apologetics for the reality of the Gospel we seek to commend will be the opportunity of an encounter with a community who have not only been radically transformed as individuals by the grace and love of Christ, but who also demonstrate what Christian community can mean as a place where all ages can meet, all kinds and conditions of human-kind be accepted, all manner of hurts and sorrows be healed. This is most effectively provided by locating a visible community of faith in each neigh-bourhood.[10]

The Cursillo movement has a significant role in many areas of the Anglican, Catholic and Uniting Churches (here in a variant form, as the *Emmaus Walk*). This lay-led movement bears witness to how powerful an effect encountering a genuinely loving community, even just over the space of three days, can have on those whose hearts cry out for such reality, but who rarely find it in their world – or in their Churches! The strength of Cursillo lies not just in its teaching and example of community but also in

Lifestyle Enclave v. Christian Community

"A lifestyle enclave is formed by people who share some features of private life. Members of a lifestyle enclave express their identity through shared patterns of appearance, consumption and leisure activities, which often serve to differentiate them sharply from those with other lifestyles. They are not interdependent, do not act together politically, and do not share a history."

Robert Bellah

its largely lay leadership, its immersion in the wider life of a diocese or denomination, and the fact that the laity involved are just rank and file church members, rather than a dedicated religious order, yet committed to change the world for Christ.

In the postmodern world, with its looseness of lifestyle and encouragement of diversity, there is still a great need for intimacy and closeness of relationships. The Church can show how this is possible through Jesus Christ. The success over recent decades of the house group movement surprisingly came at a time when modernity was at its peak, when supposedly Man had no further need of God, and the autonomous individual should not have required the close fellowship and support of others. But as the 20th century moved towards its end, society became even more secular, anonymous, and dislocated. In reaction to modernity, postmodernity affirmed community over individuality – but offered no realistic way of achieving this.

The Christian Church has the opportunity of touching society at a vital point here. A generation ago, sociologist Peter Berger wrote of a priest working in a slum area of a European city who, when asked why he chose to work there, replied: "so that the rumour of God may not disappear completely."[11]

Our worship and liturgies
Church services – their style and content – will also need close inspection in

Liturgical Renewal

"Of course there are dangers in new liturgical directions. We may take a wrong turn if we think that all we need is louder guitars, stroboscopic light, religious fashion parades. It is not a question of importing light and colour from the outside, but re-establishing a holy liturgy where the architecture and the dramaturgy – with its icons, words and music – tell again, and again and again, the old, old story."[12]

Andrew Walker

the light of the changing ways in which new generations are communicating. "In this world where icons proliferate but are profane; where texts swarm everywhere but have lost their sting; where images dominate our senses but mirror each other, liturgy is a beacon to show the way out", writes Andrew Walker.[13] First, this will involve taking far more account of the differing needs of different places, as well as the varying needs within any one community. Even now some desire eucharistic worship, others demand intergenerational services, many younger Christians appreciate teaching occasions, those unschooled in traditional liturgies look for worship in modern idiom, most welcome the imaginative use of music, dance, drama and symbolism.

Rethinking of liturgy will more often than not begin at the level of the local church, where the raw material of a postmodern world is most immediately encountered. But before the end of the 20th century even cathedrals and significant national religious celebrations were having to face up to this challenge.

The funeral of the Princess of Wales in Westminster Abbey by deliberate decision incorporated the formal and the casual, pop singer Elton John along with the ethereal singing of the traditional choir, contemporary poetry as well as Scripture reading, candles lit and held by the watching crowds in Hyde Park complementing the ceremonial robes and ritual of the clergy procession inside the Abbey. Millions were held spellbound through the medium of television bringing this worship into their own homes.

Charismatic Christianity

"Charismatic Christianity has brought back something of divine drama to the Churches, with its religion of miraculous encounter and experience. But it has been fed on interior pietism, anthropocentric prayers and private feelings for too long. In this sense it has been thoroughly modern. The postmodern world...will trust narrative more than feelings, looking for truth in 'forms of life' rather than individual experience. Liturgy both provides the visual and oral content of a living story and reconnects us to the historic tradition. Religious experience that runs ahead of the story, and hence away from it, ends up as 'charismania' – fey, orphic, deluded."[14]

Andrew Walker

Liturgy is the bringing together of the past, the present and the future, not in one perpetual present as postmodernity knows it, but in a way that shows their continuity, connectedness and application to human hopes and dreams. As the root and core of worship then, there will be the retention of the drama of the liturgy, in one sense without apology while in another sense with critical review of all we have come to take for granted as 'the way it has always been done'.

This rethinking will include our visual messages, the ceremonial robes of our worship leaders, the language our services employ, the place of liturgical movement and drama that neither underplays nor overstates, the Church's obligation to the received texts, memorable public reading of the Scriptures, the quality and applicability of all our teaching, the choice and nature of music in our worship. The goal is that the metanarrative we defiantly continue to adhere to, even in the face of its rejection by postmodernity, that grand story of the grace of God, constantly seeps through in every aspect of our formal or informal liturgies to renew the faith and life of worshippers.

Rethinking our worship will also mean seeking an appropriate balance

Bishops' Mitres:
Now Inappropriate Symbols of Christendom?

Has the time now come for a critical review of the continuing appropriateness of the mitre as the ceremonial headdress of a bishop, widely used, for example, in the Anglican Communion? This episcopal practice has in fact a comparatively recent history. The mitre was developed in the 9th century on the continent of Europe first as a symbol of office for abbots in their role as heads of monasteries. It was not until the 10th century that it became the mark of office for a bishop in the Western Church (but never to this day in the Eastern Church). The Pope then insisted that all bishops who owned allegiance to him wore the mitre as a sign of submission to his authority.

Late in the 11th century William the Conqueror introduced the mitre to the Church in the British Isles, where it had not been known or used before this time (despite many stained glass church windows depicting the first British bishops in mitres, even as early as Cuthbert, Aidan and Ninian).

The 16th century Reformation in England terminated the use of the mitre by Anglican bishops for over 300 years. Then late in the 19th century some bishops in the Church of England began to resume wearing the mitre. The first use of a mitre by an Archbishop of Canterbury since the Reformation did not occur until 1929, when Cosmo Lang adopted this style.

In 1996, speaking in Norway, the Primus of the Scottish Episcopal (Anglican) Church, Archbishop Richard Holloway, suggested that bishops attending the Lambeth Conference in 1998 should throw their mitres into the River Thames as a dramatic sign of their desire to free the Church of 'prelatical pomposity'! He invited the Lutheran bishops present to join in "this mass drowning of mitres...[so] we can move into a simpler, more Christ-like understanding of the Church."

Rehabilitating the Past and the Future through the Liturgy

"To be part of the Church is to be related through liturgy, both with the past and with the future, in a positive way. In this climate, the Church and its clergy are carriers of a culture, but a culture of the future as well as of the past – the 'culture' of the Kingdom for whose coming we pray. The Church's responsibility for preserving catholicity means we must embrace the past, the present and the future. In this way, the Church and its clergy have a distinctive role in being answerable for something more than the problems or the fashions of the moment."[15]

Anglican Board of Ministry, UK

between freedom and discipline in the services we provide for each place and occasion. The freedom will be that which enables enthusiasm to express itself in the presence of God; the discipline that which accepts the restraints of an agreed liturgy.

"Without enthusiasm, it is difficult to see Christianity surviving in the future, but if that enthusiasm is not harnessed by liturgy, communities will not learn to indwell the story and become holy. They will live on the edge of their seats, in a state of expectant anxiety, for the next and bigger wave of excitement to sweep them away."[16]

However, the postmodern reaction against set, uniform texts is likely to require denominations such as the Anglican Church to become much more flexible in trusting to their clergy and lay worship leaders the production and adaptation of local liturgies that match particular needs and congregations. This will require more and better training of those who lead worship, so that they can discern what will meet the needs of any occasion in a way that honours God while at the same time deepening the faith of the congregation. Furthermore, the emerging of a new generation largely uncomfortable with books in their hands as they pray will require worship styles that are less dependent on reading and more dependent on memory or intuition. In the 21st century Prayer Books may well come to be seen as another outgrown symbol of the era of Christendom.

Strengths Of Traditional Churches

A case study: the Anglican way. [17]

Despite their shortcomings and certain encumbrances from the past that too often hold them back and distort their mission, traditional Churches also have some potential strengths that, perhaps surprisingly, may serve them well in the changing climate created by postmodernity.

First there is the very fact of *their rootedness in the past.* This may not appeal directly to the postmodern person whose life is lived consciously in a perpetual present. But it will more readily give those who do become part of such a Church an identity and a confidence in who they are that will equip them for living in an age which has lost most awareness of its distant roots and suffers considerable anomie.

"I will open my mouth in a parable:
I will reveal the hidden meaning of things in the past,
things we have heard and known:
and such as our forbears have told us.
We will not hide them from their children,
but declare them to the next generation:...
that their posterity might know it, the children yet unborn:
and these in turn should arise and tell their children."

Psalm 78: 2-6, *A New Zealand Prayer Book*

Along with the perception that here there still lingers a body of people who care deeply for the past, there will also be seen a Church that has complete freedom to adapt to the present (e.g., in the ordination of women, revision of its liturgies, evolving roles of clergy and laity, an openness to learn from other disciplines, etc.). Anglican Christians, for example, cannot afford to forfeit the legacy bequeathed by their forebears in faith, but also must not fail to demonstrate their ability to take seriously the present and its different needs.

For a Church such as the Anglican Communion, an *episcopal system of oversight* allows for variety while sustaining unity, affirms difference while enabling community, and has developed skills to deal creatively with diversity without being threatened by it. This means enjoying a unity that is focussed in its bishops rather than in its rules of membership, in this way allowing for a looseness of association which at times in the past may have been the bane of the Church, but under postmodernity could well prove its strength.

No absolute demands other than baptism are made of those who wish to be members of the Anglican Church. It imposes no doctrinal criteria on individual members, and owns its faith as a corporate expression rather than a personal commitment. At baptism or in the renewal of baptismal vows, the two occasions alone where personal faith is required to be expressed by the candidate and/or those sponsoring the candidate, the form of faith used is the Apostles' Creed, which begins: "I believe... " However, when the Church meets as the body of baptized believers, e.g., at the Eucharist, the form of faith used in most of the new Anglican eucharistic liturgies is the Nicene Creed, which begins: "We believe..."

So, as a Church, Anglican Christians do not lay great store by developed doctrinal statements that have had to be hammered out on the anvil of rationality, other than those creeds of historic Christianity that have served the universal Church for over 1500 years. Anglican faith and belief is enshrined and expressed in its liturgy and worship. It is a Church for whom indeed *orare est credere* (to pray is to believe). This also may come to be seen as sitting well with the new spirit of postmodernity.

Another strength is a *theology* that in both its worship and order expresses the paradox of a God who is an Undivided Trinity,[18] a God who is both transcendent and immanent, a God who is apart from creation yet incarnate within creation, a God who is wholly 'other' while totally committed to the world we know.

The strongly Trinitarian nature of Anglican theology also offers to the world 'mystery', an exciting and unique model of community, and a vote for a way of knowing and understanding that has further dimensions than the purely rational.

An abiding sense of the holy, which tunes in well with that openness to the beyond in all its impenetrability that is increasingly a mark of post-modernity, has always been a feature of the Anglican Church. It is particularly captured in distinctive features of architecture and determinedly God-centred liturgies that universally have been a mark of the Anglican way. The generation shaped by late modernity were not irresistibly drawn to church buildings that they did not experience as functional auditoriums, or to church services that seemed locked into ancient formulas and rituals. But as a different wave of sensibility moves across the Western world, these very same features may offer their own, unexpected, saving grace to a Church sometimes struggling to find its identity in changing times. On their own however – without life and vitality – old ways, architecture caught in a time-warp and set formulas of worship will achieve little. The postmodern will also be looking for that which 'speaks real'.

There is also the contribution by the best of traditional Christianity, the Anglican Church no less than others, of an emphasis on an *holistic way of being Christian* that balances word and sacrament, concern for the natural world alongside the welfare of humanity, the hope of heaven together with appreciation of planet earth. This long established respect for the whole created order has taken interesting forms (e.g., pets' services, the blessing of a fishing fleet, prayers on civic and national occasions), but it has also enabled a good working relationship over many generations between science and religion at their interface, and between environmentalists and evangelists in their complementary concerns. This traces back to a concept of redemption derived from the Scriptures that is cosmic in its embrace.[19]

Further to this, within similar older Churches there is a way of understanding and handling *the Scriptures* that accords them divine authority without lapsing into bibliolatry or literalness.[20] Such Churches in their discipline of public worship provide for the regular balanced public reading of Scripture so that the Bible is heard as story – both the grand overarching story of God's relationship to humanity from the earliest beginning, and the many particular stories of the people of God in the past through whom we discover the word of God for us today.

Commitment to the local area in which a church is placed is also a feature of traditional Churches such as the Anglican Church. While 'gathered' Churches may be having much success, and are advocated by some as the way ahead for all Christians in the 21st century, especially in urban areas, there is a tradition (expressed in the parish system, despite its shortcomings) of each local Anglican church 'owning' the district around it, i.e., identifying with its ethos, its pains and pleasures, its hopes and hardships. For example, the bishops of the Anglican Diocese of Wellington have committed themselves to ensure that quality worship and Christian ministry is available in even the remotest areas of this large diocese, wherever Christians in a rural district desire and are prepared to support such worship and ministry. This is the doctrine of the incarnation expressed in ecclesiology. And it offers a hopeful window for the future, even if the parish system as it has developed is no longer in every situation the most appropriate way of expressing this commitment to the people of an area.

This sense of being a Church identifying strongly with the local community, a further echo of those early Celtic roots of much of British Christianity, is balanced by another potential strength of the older style Churches for a postmodern world – their readiness to admit and affirm the status and strengths of other Churches who have different histories and ways of being Christian, as also part of a much wider, global family of Christian Churches.

This in turn leads to an acceptance of a measure of diversity in how the Church locally will express itself. Comprehensiveness has for many years been a feature of the Anglican way. This is a Church which has learned to manage difference without division, and to accept people discounted by the rest of society, painful as this sometimes may be for the Church in working through what this means for its life and order.

An appreciation of the *value of the visual* is a further promising feature in the Anglican Church. This has the potential of speaking engagingly to postmodern generations in the 21st century. It will be appreciated the more if it is encountered not as a gimmick, a publicity trick to get in touch with

Human Sexuality

One point of pain for the Church in several areas of the world during the final decades of the 20th century has been the question of homo-sexuality, and the hospitality that can be extended by the Church to gay and lesbian people. The deep feelings aroused have not been helped by the attitudes and actions of some advocates at both extremes of the issue (who in the end, often quite unknowingly, do more harm than good to the positions they hold and the courses they propose the Church should take). Nor has the debate been assisted by confusing what the Church minimally expects of its lay membership with the higher expec-tations it has of its ordained clergy. A generosity of outlook in the spirit of Jesus Christ requires that all and any who seek to draw near to Christ should be able to do so within the supportive fellowship of his body, the Church; yet leadership within the Church has always and in various ways required those seeking ordination to meet criteria not demanded of the laity. In the New Testament the Pastoral Epistles major on distinctive requirements of those who are to be set aside as teachers and presbyters of the Church of God.

a new generation, or as an overblown expression of eccentricity conveying more about the nature of the Constantinian Church in the 4th century, or the excesses of 19th century Tractarianism. It needs to be transparently about the glory and wonder of the gospel of Jesus Christ, met as time-tested and constantly reshaped church architecture, decoration or ritual that has been developed over many centuries in response to the changing world.

Use of the colours of the season, with a style and panache that fits the times; the subtle background of stained glass memorials, hopefully without retaining all of the saccharine sentiment of the Victorian era; sensitive use of the art of banner-making and displaying; restrained use of robes and ritual appropriate to the place and the occasion; liturgy used as participatory drama; music that unites and envelops the visual and the verbal in an aura

The Challenge to the Christian Church

"For Christians, theological clarity and devotional intensity are important, but in and of themselves, they will not be enough. Christian understanding must also proceed through self-conscious awareness of the subtle ways in which modernity affects faith and life. Christian understanding must further proceed with imagination about how the Christian community can maintain integrity to biblical revelation and to the legacy of Christian witness through the centuries. It is here that we find the structural antidote to the pressures of modernity."[21]

James D. Hunter

of worship – all this can come more easily to Christians who are determined neither to discard entirely the heritage they have received from the past nor to capitulate totally to the mood of the present age.

Where can we begin – and how? The way ahead lies neither in embracing without reservation the heterogeneity admired by the postmodern spirit (not least because this fails to take seriously enough the fresh crises of identity this is likely to create), nor in clawing back uncritically selective traditions and values of a past, premodern ideal. Rather does the future lie in rediscovering the ancient historic core to the faith while enabling that same story, transported by the Scriptures down the ages, to take up residence in our contemporary Western world, the world of postmodernity. "What we are now seeing, as we approach the third millennium, is the failure of principled humanism to convince the modern world that it has a more believable story to live by than the older stories it has replaced."[22]

Christian Challenges to Postmodernity

At certain points, the Christian Church will find itself having firmly to part company with postmodernity and respectfully to say: "Here we stand; we can do no other." Such points of unease with the temper of postmodernity are likely to be:

1. Postmodernity's propensity for *collapsing the past and the future into the present*. It is of the very nature of our faith and of our understanding of the real which we have come to know through God that there is a past that we need to continue to respect and a future that we need to endeavour to understand. Life for the Christian can not be the perpetual present of postmodernity. Worship, the heart of the life of the Christian Church, particularly the eucharist, serves as a week by week rediscovery of a past that has given our lives meaning, realization of a present that we are called to go out into now as disciples of Christ, and reminder of a future that we can only anticipate eagerly. The challenge is to commend this way of knowing and looking to a world which, under the pressures of postmodernity, is constantly being encouraged to see things differently.

2. The postmodern *pessimism and hopelessness in looking outside the present*. We need to recognize the causes for such an outlook on the part of those who have experienced only the environment of a postmodern world. Here again, a gospel of hope, of there being another way of reading our current condition, of an outlook that is grounded in the person of the One of whom it was said: "Jesus Christ, the same yesterday, today and for ever", this good news will be the response we will want to make in every way possible.[23]

3. Postmodern *rejection of metanarrative of any kind*. Let us readily recognise that many of the grand accounts of the world and how it may be released from its pain have not rung true – the Marxist story of economic salvation, the modernist story of rational management of our lives and societies, the Freudian story of liberation through introspection, the scientific story of problem-solving through strict application of the scientific method.

   But let us also invite another look at God's story, as preserved in the Scriptures and lived out in the life of Jesus Christ – a story that all too often has been lost by the Church under a confusing mass of hesitations and qualifications, or concealed beneath a foliage of ritual and beyond-shelf-life traditions. We need to show this as a story that is worth listening to again, as a story that makes more sense than the others, as a story in which we are able to hold together:

- both recognition of the potential good in every one of us – and our potential for evil;
- both a sense of pessimism about the future when considered in purely human terms – and a confident optimism once we have brought God into the equation;
- both the opportunity to live life to the full now (with all the joys and delights and realism of suffering which this entails) – and the call to look to another life of another kind at a time beyond this present time;
- both respect for the impressive contributions of science and technology – and a refusal to fall meekly under their tyranny.

4. Bizarre *alternative religiosities* spawned by postmodernity. We cannot support the kind of generosity that accepts any form of religiosity. However, we will make this point not by way of heavy-handed condemnation of contemporary neo-paganism and New Age consciousness, but by tendering a faith and a spirituality that makes better 'gospel sense', even to a postmodern person, when placed alongside these revivals of ancient religious beliefs. The Christian faith when told clearly and lived out visibly will have its own convincing power.

5. Postmodernity's *make-believe worlds of virtual reality*. As Christians, we will want to challenge postmodernity over its idea of the real, and its belief that we have the power to create our own trouble-free worlds of virtual reality.

    We will do this, again, not so much by open confrontation as by demonstrating in our own multitude of local churches how one can live with dignity, joy and peace in the unkind world of our times, "for better for worse, for richer for poorer, in sickness and in health." We will endeavour to re-create the life of the disciples of Christ in every neighbourhood and district, expressed in worshipping communities that have as their *raison d'être* God's glory rather than Man's desires. And closer inspection hopefully will show this to be no fantasy.

6. The *insistence on entertainment*. This has become a characteristic of postmodern times, even in worship. We will offer an alternative to religious entertainment – worship that thrills the soul without selling

out to the meretricious, that warms the heart without having also to tickle the fancy, that sharpens the mind but not at the price of dulling the brain, that deploys visual arts, dramatic movement, and quality music yet without benefit of pop stars or stage idols.

7. The inclination of a postmodern generation to look for *meaning in sign and surface*. Our persistent Christian faith will want to show that there is more to meaning than surface appearance or the signs postmoderns create to communicate in their world. For example, each person will continue to be known and honoured by a name given in baptism, as an individual with personal value to God and to his or her fellow believers. The Christian Church will continue to offer to each local community by its presence in each area or suburb a soul, a name, a *persona*, by identifying with the hopes and the hurts, the faded history and the future ambitions of that place. At the same time the role of the Church in each local district will be to help that community feel good about itself, to serve as a haven for its healing, a centre for its celebrations, a repository for its memories. In ways like these, the Church will persist in rebutting postmodernity's growing obsession with superficial sign and image.

8. Postmodernity's preference for *mobility and lack of commitment*. Modernity so undermined old ways and ancient institutions that public respect for them and therefore any sense of abiding commitment to them was lost – the Church and its ministers, marriage and morality, the authority of schoolteachers, at times even the police and the army. This spilled over to affect society in its totality – church-going became no longer a duty but a matter of choice. Keeping a marriage together came to be seen as dependent on how much it suited the convenience of each of the two parties involved; divorce became more frequent; a young man who got a girl pregnant felt no necessary sense of continuing obligation towards her; a woman who found herself with an unwanted pregnancy saw this as an unwelcome intrusion before which her personal well-being and freedom came first. Even Christians became slack about openly owning allegiance to one Christian denomination or becoming committed to a particular local church through its good times and bad.

Under postmodernity, while there is a swing back to the community or group and its needs away from a narrowly personal view of faith and meaning, the footlooseness acquired during late modernity persists. Commitment is at a premium still. Christians will want to stand against this casualness of relationship and to recover the value of costly commitment in every area of life, from church membership to membership of the local sports club. The cross of Christ under which we place ourselves in any century will allow us to do no other.

Four Options for the Future

In his book *The Church Confident*[24], Leander Keck suggests there are four possibilities before the Christian Church in its response to what seems to many an increasingly hostile world:

1. *To go counter-cultural.* But this is really not a viable option for mainline Churches who by nature are committed to whatever society they are located in, whatever its state.

2. *To be resident aliens.* That is to say, having more concern to be real than to be pure, while at the same time taking our heartbeat from the tempo of the Bible rather than from the world and its incessant rhythms.

   This is the course advocated by Willimon and Hauerwas in their book *Resident Aliens*. It is also the course proposed by Andrew Walker, who writes: "There will be no future for the broad Church in a postmodern world. We will have to return to structures...akin to the monastery, the religious community and the sect...If...the world staggers onwards with more consumption, wrapped up in mass culture yet splitting at the seams, we will still need to create sectarian plausibility structures in order for our story to take hold of our congregations and root them in the gospel handed down by our forebears." [25]

   This could leave us with a Church very like the old missionary compounds, a world within a world.

3. *To be socially active.* Here the Church identifies society as the place where God is principally at work, and where the calling of the Church is to recognize and cooperate with this already active work of God in reshaping

Social Justice

"Activist Christians who talk much about justice promote a notion of justice that envisions a society in which faith in God is rendered quite unnecessary, since everyone already believes in peace and justice even when everyone does not believe in God."[26]

Hauerwas and Willimon

society. But this presents a utilitarian view of the Church and its role, a view that sees everything in terms of benefits.

4. *To be committed both to the Gospel and to the world.* This suggests dual citizenship in which the Churches neither expect to re-establish a theocracy, nor seek to withdraw from the mainstream of public life,[27] but, as with salt, exercise a continuing influence in an invisible way on their society through "engagement without captivity".

John Habgood, the former Archbishop of York, describes this as 'critical solidarity'. "'Solidarity' implies a willingness to be sympathetic towards the needs and aims of society, and the responsibilities of those in power. 'Critical' preserves the duality, the necessary distancing from power if the Church is to be true to itself...It is an expression of the Anglican ethos which has always...emphasised that faith has to be lived out, both personally and corporately, in the context of daily life. The aim is neither to withdraw from the world, nor simply to accept it, but to work for its transformation through the presence and power of Christ."[28] Such a relationship involves both affirmation and critique,[29] prudence and passion.

It also raises the question as to the relative importance Christians can give to 'the nation' in which they live, when its claims and loyalties conflict with their duty to God and membership of the Kingdom of God. Here again, it may well be that the first three centuries of church history yield more guidance in this matter than the last three centuries.

A Public Truth

"The Gospel is not anything we choose, or the bits we enjoy, or those elements that affirm modern sensibility. It is the Church's grand narrative, which is essential not only for its own identity but for the salvation of the world. However, to insist on this is to incur the wrath of contemporary thinking. One of the features of life in an advanced industrial society is that absolute claims of any kind are anathema. This is why Christianity is tolerated by secularists as private opinion, but not what Lesslie Newbigin has called 'public truth'."[30]

Two Roles for the Church

Keck also offers two roles for the Church in such a scenario in this new century:

The first is the role of public theologian – discerning, interpreting, affirming or challenging the deepest impulses of our society, e.g., the continuing modernist assumptions that plague our education system concerning individual potential and inherent human goodness. "By unmasking the illusions about ourselves, the Churches can be a positive influence on the mindset of the nation and thereby mitigate the frustration and despair that comes from expecting the impossible of ourselves."[31] Lesslie Newbigin sees the unmasking of ill-founded assumptions of modernity as a basic task of the Christian concerned with society today. "Any mind shaped by modernity will be fully furnished with beliefs and assumptions which seem to make Christian faith untenable or at least very questionable. Part of Christian testimony is to uncover the hidden assumptions behind these beliefs."[32]

Also the Church can provide a plausibility structure, a commonly accepted "legitimating story or myth, which expresses the people's identity and place in the world." This is what many modern societies lack today. High-sounding Western abstractions about 'humanity' are no substitute.

The second is the role of **nurturer of quality leadership** – by the

Churches nourishing strong leaders, whether male or female. This is likely to mean the Church being more hospitable to people with strong egos, and exceptional charisma, claims Leander Keck.[33] If Christian ministry does not call them, they will still be well prepared to exercise leadership at other levels of society. And those who do so serve will need to be continually nourished on the Great Story, in defiance of postmodern rejection of all metanarrative, in order to maintain in sharp focus Gospel lenses through which to view the world and their responsibilities in it.

This in turn will call for a generation of preachers and teachers, ordained or lay, who have not only the gift to understand both the word of God and the world of people, but the prophetic ability to relate the one to the other.

The mana accompanying leadership will have to be far more earned than expected. "Religious leaders in the Western world are no longer authority figures, but are perceived to be vestiges of an earlier culture in which religion counted. They are therefore anachronisms, to be treated with the respect reserved for extinct species."[34]

This accounts also for much of the clerical malaise that has been a feature of the last two decades of the 20th century. Leadership even at the level of the parish has been affected as ordained ministry has been cut adrift from the safety net of what is meaningful and valuable in society. "This has created a sense of uneasiness that has settled over the work of ministers like a thick fog. The discomfort and ambiguity that ministers experience are just two of the many consequences of the growing secularization of the modern world. [Compared with bankers and lawyers whose place in the structures of modern society are readily recognized,] what ministers are engaged in has no institutional recognition in the public square because there are not many who recognize its relevance in that context. They and their work are constantly being pushed to the margins of society...

"There can be little doubt that it is the realization of their sinking fortunes that has inclined the clergy to give their concentrated attention to the problem of how to present themselves instead as serious professionals in the modern world...They have been obliged to define their ministry in terms of its marketability. The market has come to dominate the way in which they exercise their ministry, often taking precedence over the matters of internal calling and over personal spirituality...In this new clerical order, technical and managerial competence in the Church have plainly come to dominate the definition of pastoral service...The older role of the pastor as broker of truth has been eclipsed by the newer managerial functions."[35]

Authentic Christianity

In the briefest terms, the early decades of the 21st century call the Christian Church in the West, both the older, traditional Churches and the newer, independent congregations, to new levels of authenticity as bearers of the gospel of Jesus Christ. This will be the only adequate way to fulfil Christ's mission in a world largely shaped by the forces of modernity, but now being steadily distorted by the pressures of postmodernity. Such authenticity will in the end prove the most convincing argument for the Gospel to those still amenable to discovering a truth outside themselves. Such authenticity will prove the most arresting evidence of the Gospel for those who had given up on the Church – ancient or modern! Such authenticity will draw most powerfully those, young and old, who come to question whether there are any depths of mystery or wonder still to be found in the world beneath the surface superficialities created by the media or beyond the pleasure-measured horizons set by their easy-going peers.

Even at the height of modernity, in its raunchiest heydays, some yearning for the spiritual, for that which is beyond, was apparent. Hungry hands picked away at morsels offered by the occult and tapped at memories of old paganism still lingering around the world. The need was there – but the Church of God at that time for the most part seemed ill-equipped to answer it. The traditional Churches especially were often too preoccupied looking after their own and devizing survival mechanisms in the face of a receding tide of nominal membership. The newer congregations spent their energies dealing with surface issues and meeting presenting needs without discerning the deeper flowing changes taking place in society and intellectual thought.

When many of that generation happened to encounter the Church in its traditional form, it felt to them out of place in their kind of world, a left-over from another age, a curiosity rather than a cure. Turning to the contemporary Churches, many found these also were not relating at any depth to the world as they knew it. Only something authentic, something that they could sense and see as being indeed part of the world they belonged to, yet pointing beyond it to another, would convince and hold them.

It is this kind of authenticity that we need to aspire to and work for today. It will be an authenticity that is at one and the same time:

Authentic community – like the Christians of the first centuries, learning what it means to be a disciple of Jesus Christ in this kind of world and then living accordingly, along with all the failures and frustrations this will involve, no less so in the 21st century than in the first. Authentic community, like a beacon on a hill, will allow the light of Christ to be seen and observed, lived out in numerous defiant communities of believers, scattered over the face of the land, small and large, urban and rural, held together in the bonds of love by the person of Jesus Christ and expressed above all in the priority given to worship.

Authentic worship – that not only commands priority of place in the weekly activities of all 21st century believers, but also conveys to any who stumble upon it a feeling of wonder and awe, an immediate sense of the holiness of God, and how much this means to these people. This may well require discarding some outworn, beyond shelf-life aspects of inherited worship, and also some pseudo-copies of fads and fashions culled more from current culture than from the Gospel of grace. But it will issue in worship that unmistakably draws people into the presence of God and then sends them out in the strength of the Holy Spirit, to live as disciples of Christ. Working out the details will differ from place to place – but one criterion will judge all: is it authentic? Does it ring true?

Authentic message – in the sense of a message faithful to the Gospel as it has been conveyed to us in the Scriptures, unclouded and undiluted by extraneous other messages. How this is communicated will depend on the person, the place and the occasion. There is no call for uniformity – just for faithfulness to the word from God, for 'authenticity', for consistency between what is said and what is read.

Authentic confidence – neither that arrogance of modernity's rationalism which believed humankind was in the course of solving all its problems on its own, thank you, nor that flippancy of the postmodernist who believes life anyway is without meaning or significance other than that which each person gives to it.[36] But rather what is needed is the certainty born of encountering, through Jesus Christ and the body of his followers, the Creator God whose Spirit palpably gives life and whose Word positively yields light.

In these ways, as Christian Churches in the Western world face a new century within a critically changed environment, faith, joy and strength may once again be discovered and shared with others – and God once more be 'our hope for years to come'.

Epilogue

By Harold Turner

The DeepSight Trust welcomes this book into its first Publication Series, in the confidence that it offers an insight into the deeper cultural forces and worldviews that shape and motivate New Zealand and all other predominantly Western societies at this stage in their history.

The concentration upon Western culture is deliberate for three simple reasons:

1. That Western culture tends to become the dominant culture in all intercultural relationships, for better or for worse, and this book with its fair presentation of the pros and cons of both modernity and postmodernity should help to identify these two aspects.

2. That Western culture is the only culture that has spread to some degree into almost every part of the globe, and continues to do so, for good or for ill. It is therefore to this extent the first world culture, and an inescapable partner in all bi/multicultural situations.

3. That bi/multicultural discussions demand an in-depth understanding of each of the cultures concerned, as a prior requirement. This book has therefore offered a basic tool for further discussion between cultures. Readers may have reflected that the issues analyzed here, especially

modernism and postmodernism, are characteristic of the current Western culture within which they have arisen, but not originally of other cultures which they are reaching by importation from the West.

All authors write and all readers read from within a certain set of values or assumptions, a particular perspective, stance, or worldview, whether they are conscious of this or not. This author makes his Christian stance quite clear, while at the same time recognizing that like his fellow Christians he is affected by all aspects of Western culture, including those not congruent with the Christian worldview. Brian Carrell recognizes, however, that we are all in this Western mixture together, and therefore can identify ourselves at many points of his text.

He finds the norms for his Christian stance in the biblical story, and distinguishes this as the Gospel from the life of the Churches. Over the centuries the Church in the West has absorbed many of the incompatible elements of Western culture and itself deserves radical criticism. Nevertheless he recognizes the essential place of the Church, warts and all, in the Christian story and he writes as a loyal churchman within the Anglican tradition, the one he knows best. As his case study of this tradition in Chapter 7 shows, he also speaks to all Christians, and beyond.

The extensive use of quotations in the text indicates the vast amount of concern and self-analysis going on in our Western culture, and, more importantly, the extensive consensus that is appearing from many different starting points. Those of us struggling to survive at the many coal-faces of our society can take heart from all the back-room work that Brian Carrell has helped to bring up front.

This book is therefore a foundation publication in the DeepSight Series. It furthers the aims of the Trust to establish a major resource, research, study, and action structure for "deep insight" into Western culture and its ills. While starting in New Zealand its global manifestations must also be taken in account, along with all the other cultures. Brian Carrell's work offers us a long-lasting tool as we start on this intimidating task.

ENDNOTES

Chapter One

1   David Wells, *God in the Wasteland*, (Eerdmans/InterVarsity Press, 1994), p. 71.
2   Philip Sampson in P. Sampson, V. Samuel, & C. Sugden (eds.), *Faith and Modernity*, (Regnum,1994), p. 48.
3   TV One (NZ) Network News, 11 August 1997.
4   *The Dominion*, Wellington, 14 August 1997.
5   *The Dominion*, Wellington, 19 August 1997.
6   Michael Carr-Gregg of Melbourne's Centre for Adolescent Health, at a conference in Dunedin and reported in *The Dominion*, Wellington, 13 August 1997.
7   David Wells, *No Place for Truth*, (Eerdmans, 1993), p. 159.
8   Andrew Walker, *Telling the Story*, (SPCK, 1996), p. 168.
9   Tim Corney, Seeking Hope in the Ruins of Postmodernity, *Zadok Perspectives*, July 1995.
10 Wells, 1994, p. 99-100.
11 Lawrence Osborn, *Restoring the Vision*, (Mowbray, 1995), p. 105ff.
12 Leander Keck, *The Church Confident*, (Abingdon, 1993), p. 26.
13 See Bob Goudzwaard, *Idols of Our Time*, (InterVarsity Press, 1984).
14 Brian Walsh, *Subversive Christianity: Imaging God in a Dangerous Time*, (Regius Press, 1991), p. 27f.
15 See M. Featherstone, *Consumer Culture And Postmodernism*, (Sage, 1991).
16 Wells, 1994, p. 74.
17 Bryan Appleyard, *Understanding the Present*, (Picador, 1992), p. 79, 108.
18 Harvey Cox, *Fire From Heaven*, (Addison-Wesley, 1996), p. 119-20.
19 Nelson Mandela, *Long Walk to Freedom*, (Abacus, 1994), p. 13.
20 At the opening of the Fourth International Global Forum Conference, Kyoto, Japan, 20 April, 1993. Both observations are quoted in Howard Snyder, *EarthCurrents*, (Abingdon, 1995), p. 13.

21 Jon R. Snyder in Translator's Introduction to Gianni Vattimo, *The End of Modernity*, (Polity, 1988).
22 Mapping the Postmodern, *New German Critique* , no.33, 1984, pp. 5-52. Quoted in David Harvey, *The Condition of Postmodernity*, (Blackwell, 1990), p. 39.
23 Stanley Grenz, *A Primer on Postmodernism*, (Eerdmans, 1996), p. 10.
24 Harvey Cox, 1996, p. 104. In the 1960s, Cox wrote the popular but controversial book *The Secular City* (Penguin Books, 1968). His position has shifted significantly since then.
25 David Lyon, *Postmodernity*, (Oxford University Press, 1994), p. 85f.
26 Jane Flax, quoted in Middleton and Walsh, 1995, p. 24.
27 Middleton and Walsh, 1995, p. 25.
28 David Bosch, *Transforming Mission*, (Orbis, 1991), p. 4.
29 Grace Davie, *Religion in Britain Since 1945*, (Blackwell, 1994), p. 190.
30 Jim Wallis, *The Soul of Politics*, (Orbis, 1994), p. 5.
31 Diogenes Allen, *Christian Belief in a Postmodern World: The Full Wealth of Conviction*, (John Knox, 1989).
32 Harvey, 1990, p. vii.
33 J. Middleton and B. Walsh, *Truth Is Stranger Than It Used To Be*, (InterVarsity Press, 1995), p. 41.
34 J. Bottum, Christians and Postmoderns, *First Things*, no. 40, February 1994, p. 28f.
35 Harvey, 1990, p. 99.
36 Ed. Sampson, *et al.*, 1994, p. 7.
37 Steven Connor, *Postmodernist Culture*, (Blackwell, 1989), p. 27.
38 Kenneth Thompson in, *Modernity and Its Futures*, ed. Stuart Hall *et al.*, (Open University, 1992), p. 226-7.

Chapter Two

1   In D.S. Dockery, *The Challenge of Postmodernism*, (Bridgepoint, 1995), p. 24.

2 Walker, 1996, p. 107.
3 Neil Postman, *Technopoly: The Surrender of Culture to Technology*, (Vintage, 1993), p. 36.
4 See Grenz, 1996, pp. 60-70.
5 Grenz, 1996, p. 67.
6 Walker, 1996, p. 49.
7 Postman, 1993, p. 34.
8 Anthony Giddens, *The Consequences of Modernity*, (Polity, 1990), p. 4.
9 Krishan Kumar, *From Post-Industrial to Post-Modern Society*, (Blackwell, 1995), p. 82.
10 *The Times* (London), 29 October 1996.
11 Philip Sampson in ed. Sampson *et al.*, 1993, p. 33.
12 Walker, 1996, p. 106-7.
13 Wells, 1994, p. 7-9.
14 Zygmunt Bauman, *Life in Fragments*, (Blackwell, 1995), p. 5.
15 Walker, 1996, p. 155.
16 Wells, 1994, p. 29.
17 Wells, 1993, p.167.
18 See Wells, 1994, chapter 3.
19 See Drusilla Scott, *Everyman Revived: The Commonsense of Michael Polanyi*, (The Book Guild, 1985; Eerdmans, 1995).
20 Quoted in Walker, 1996, p. 57.
21 Lesslie Newbigin, *A Word in Season*, (Eerdmans/St Andrews, 1994), chapter 9.
22 Walker, 1996, p. 57.
23 Tom Sine, *Wild Hope*, (Word, 1991), p. 252.
24. David Lyon, *Future Society*, 1984, p. 30.
25 Sampson, 1994, p. 40-1.
26 Wells, 1994, p. 202.
27. Wells, 1994, p. 14.
28 John Polkinghorne, *Quarks, Chaos and Christianity*, (Triangle, 1994), p. 57.
29 James D. Hunter in ed. Sampson, *et al.*, 1994, p. 17.
30 In *The Sunday Times* (London), 3 November, 1996.
31 Richard J. Neuhaus, *The Naked Public Square*, (Eerdmans, 1986).
32 C. Ben Mitchell in Dockery, 1995, p. 274.
33 Robert Bellah, *Habits of the Heart: Individualism and Commitment in American Life*, (University of California Press, 1985), p. 221.
34 Wells, 1993, p. 83-4.
35 Grenz, 1996, p. 80-1.
36 Middleton and Walsh, 1995, p. 15-17.
37 Genesis 11 : 1-9.
38 *Silver Kris*, November 1996, p. 44-46.
39 Middleton and Walsh, 1995, p. 19

Chapter Three

1 Charles Taylor, *The Malaise of Modernity*, (Anansi Press, 1991).
2 Walker, 1996, p. 151.
3 James D. Hunter, in ed. Sampson *et al.*, 1995, p. 18-20.
4 James D. Hunter, in ed. Sampson *et al.*, 1995, p. 19.
5 Lyon, 1994, p. 23.
6 Lyon, 1994, p. 23.
7 Max Weber, *The Protestant Ethic and the Spirit of Capitalism*, (Scribner's, 1958).
8 Distinction needs to be drawn between *secular, secularism* and *secularization*; also between *secularism* as understood in the USA, in the United Kingdom, in France, and in countries such as Australia and New Zealand; and yet again between how *secular* was used in the 1960s, and its use 30 years later. See David Lyon, Secularization: the Fate of Faith in Modern Society, *Themelios*, 10(1), September 1984, p. 14f; and Peter Berger, From the Crisis of Religion to the Crisis of Secularity, in *The Ethics of Authenticity*, (Harvard University Press, 1991). Martin Marty has argued that secularism has followed different courses in Europe and Britain compared with America. He claims that in the USA secularism coexists with religion, whereas in Europe it rejects religion, while in Britain, secularism largely ignores it.
9 Lyon, 1994, p. 32. Some writers refer to this as the 'McDonaldization' of Western societies.
10 Zygmunt Bauman, *Intimations of Postmodernity*, (Routledge, 1992), p. 225-6.
11 Postman, 1993, p. 87.
12 *The Sunday Times* (London), 3 November 1996
13 Robert Bellah, Cultural Barriers to the Understanding of the Church and its Public role, *Missiology*, 19(4), October 1991, pp. 461-73.
14 *The Times* (London), 30 October 1996, p. 18.
15 Whereas *alienation* is considered an appropriate metaphor for the identity established by modernity, it is suggested that *schizophrenia* is a truer description under the conditions of postmodernity.
16 *Anomie* means the loss of *nomos* or order, meaning and identity. Quoted in Middleton and Walsh, 1995, p. 36.

175

17 Wells, 1994, p. 97f.
18 *The Times* (London), 29 October 1996.
19 *The Times* (London), 31 October 1996, p. 20. The Labour Leader, Tony Blair, four days later in reference to this issue of morality as a political issue in the lead-up to a General Election, made clear that his party, which had been making a strong plug for a new era of social morality, in no way advocated a highly regulated society in the area of ethics. He said: "We reject not tolerance but extreme libertarianism." *The Times* (London), 4 November 1996
20 Roger Lundin, *The Culture of Interpretation*, (Eerdmans, 1993) p. 249.
21 Wells, 1994, p. 94.
22 Wells, 1993, p. 183.
23 R. Kew and R.J. White, *New Millennium, New Church*, (Cowley, 1992), p. 152.
24 G.E. Veith, The New Tribalism. *Postmodern Times: A Christian Guide to Contemporary Thought and Culture*, (Crossway Books, 1994).
25 Chris Rojek, *Decentering Leisure*, (Sage, 1995), p. 151-2.
26 Sabino Acquaviva, *The Decline of the Sacred in Industrial Society*, (Blackwells, 1979).
27 *The Times* (London), 12 October 1996.
28 Middleton and Walsh, 1995, p.14-15.
29 Editorial in *The Times* (London), 29 October 1996.
30 Veith, 1994, p. 145.
31 Comment by Michael Ignatieff interviewing Charles Taylor (McGill University and Université de Montreal) recorded in *The Listener* (UK), March 20, 1986, p. 16f.
32 Walter Brueggemann, *Biblical Perspectives on Evangelism*, (Abingdon, 1993).
33 Referred to by Lyon, 1994, p. 12.
34 Quoted in J. Middleton and B. Walsh, *The Transforming Vision*, (InterVarsity Press, 1984), p. 9.

Chapter Four

1 Giddens, 1990, p. 48.
2 Cited in ed. Sampson, *et al.*, 1994, p. 29.
3 Harvey, 1990, p. 38f.
4 Hans Bertens, *The Idea of the Postmodern*, (Routledge,1995), p. 111.
5 Grenz, 1996, p. 38.
6 For an evaluation of Nietzsche's contribution to the shaping of the postmodern mind, see Anthony Thistelton, On Meaning, Manip-

ulation and Promise, *Interpreting God and the Postmodern Self*, (T. & T. Clark, 1995).
7 An observation by Os Guinness, *The Grave-digger File*, (Hodder & Stoughton, 1983), p. 94.
8 Graham Cray, *The Gospel and Tomorrow's Culture*, (Church Pastoral Aid Society, 1994), p. 72.
9 Middleton and Walsh, 1995, chapter 4.
10 Grenz, 1996, p. 59.
11 Newbigin, 1994, p. 101.
12 Middleton and Walsh, 1995, p. 83.
13 Frederic Jameson, *Postmodernism and Consumer Society*, (Verso, 1991), p. 125.
14 Veith, 1994, p. 146.
15 Quoted in Harvey, 1990, p. 44.
16 Jean Baudrillard, *The Precession of Simulacra*, 1981.
17 Featherstone, 1991, p. 124.
18 Jameson, 1991, p. 18.
19 Harvey, 1990, p. 284.
20 Harvey, 1990, p. 54.
21 M. Featherstone, in *Mapping the Futures*, ed. Bird, (Routledge, 1993), p. 170-1.
22 Dick Hebdidge, *Hiding in the Light*, (Routledge, 1988).
23 David Harvey, *Looking Backwards on Postmodernism*, (Blackwell, 1990).
24 Ed. Sampson, *et al.*, 1994, p. 37.
25 Rachel Campbell-Johnston in *The Times* (London), 12 October, 1996, p. 18.
26 Middleton and Walsh, 1995, p. 31-2.
27 Lyon, 1994, p. 46.
28 Philippa Berry and A. Wernick (eds.), *Shadow of Spirit: Postmodernism and Religion*, (Routledge, 1992) p. 3.
29 John Drane, *Evangelism for a New Age*, (Marshall Pickering, 1994).
30 Ed. Sampson *et al.*, 1994, p. 38.
31 Zygmunt Bauman, *Life in Fragments*, (Blackwell, 1995), p. 24.
32 Kew and White, 1992, p. 134-7.
33 1930 Lambeth Conference.
34 Newbigin, 1994, chapter 10.
35 Walker, 1996, p. 118.
36 A term used by Richard Dawkins in his book, *The Selfish Gene*. In *The Origins of Virtue*, Viking, 1996, Matt. Ridley writes of "humankind's propensity for self-interest", while in *The Sunday Times* (London, 3 November 1996) a reviewer of Stephen Jay Gould's *Life's Grandeur*, Cape, 1996, says: "Our fondly cherished illusion of the perfectibility of living forms through Darwinian

natural selection is the straw man...Gould flattens and finally pulverizes."

37 Andrew Walker, 1996, p. 103-4, notes: "...the writer Saul Bellow recently wrote of American society: 'For the first time probably in the history of the Republic, parents doubt that their children will live as good a life as they have done.' "

38 Robert N. Bellah, writing in *Postmodern Theology: Christian Faith in a Pluralist World,* ed. Fred. Burnham, (San Francisco, 1989), p. 77, states: [At best] "we are Newtonians in an Einsteinian world, even in a post Einsteinian world!...We unconsciously believe in a world of endless uniform extension in time and space. But the world of contemporary physics is one in which space and time are curved, have a beginning, and probably an end."

39 In Burnham (ed.), The Emerging Postmodern World, *Postmodern Theology: Christian Faith in a Pluralist World,* (San Francisco, 1989).

40 Harvey, 1990, p 40.

Chapter Five

1 Featherstone, 1991, p. 8.
2 Grenz, 1996, p. 23.
3 Quoted in Harvey, 1990, p. 21.
4 Grenz, 1996, p. 35.
5 Harvey, 1990, p. 63.
6 Wells, 1994, p. 48.
7 Ed. Sampson, *et al.*, 1994, p. 39.
8 C. Longley, in the Foreword to Jonathan Sachs, *Faith in the Future*, (Darton, Longman & Todd, 1995).
9 Wells, 1993, p. 161.
10 Walker, 1996, p. 104.
11 Bosch, 1991, p. 349.
12 Wells, 1993, p. 287.
13 Giddens, 1990, p. 3, 149ff.
14 In David Dockery, *The Challenge of Postmodernism*, (BridgePoint, 1995), p. 25f., 82.
15 Dockery, 1995, p. 395.
16 Bertens, 1995, p. 248.
17 Grenz, 1996, p. 45.
18 Middleton and Walsh, 1995, p. 109-10.
19 Bertens, 1995, p. 247.
20 Walker, 1996, p. 173. Or is this another example of 'biting the hand that has fed you'? The Christian Church knows what this is like, after its experience of founding universities, promoting schools, establishing hospitals, and pioneering radical social service work – and then being progressively shut out of each of them in turn. It was not long before another generation grew up "who knew not Joseph". Exodus 1: 8.

21 Cf., Oscar Wilde's acerbic comment that he sensed was true even at the beginning of this century: "Work is the curse of the drinking class."

22 Lyon, 1994, p. 68.
23 Walker, 1996, p. 107. He also acknowledges "an accelerating pace of cultural change since the 1960s (p. 139)."

24 Walker, 1996, p. 143-6.
25 It was Charles Revlon who said: "In the laboratory I make cosmetics. In the store I sell dreams."

26 Wells, 1994, p. 219-20.
27 Christopher Lasch, *The Minimal Self: Psychic Survival in Troubled Times*, (W.&W. Norton, 1985).

28 Wells, 1993, p. 46.
29 Walker, 1996, p. 150.
30 *North and South* (Auckland), April 1997, p. 108.

31 Sampson, 1994, p. 31.
32 Harvey, 1990, p. 159.
33 For the way in which 'infotainment' as a way of communication has greatly affected political style, church worship, teaching in the classroom, news presentation etc., see Neil Postman, *Amusing Ourselves to Death*, (Methuen, 1987).

34 Peter Berger in ed. Sampson, *et al.*, 1994, p. 8.

35 Lyon, 1994, p. 57: "Not just artistic and consumer goods, but also intellectual and even religious ones become subject to the market, which resists both monopoly and hierarchy."

36 See Lyon, 1994, p. 39.
37 Middleton and Walsh, 1995, p. 55.
38 *New Internationalist*, December 1996, p. 18-19.

39 Article in *InfoTech Weekly*, a supplement in *The Dominion* (Wellington), 16 February 1998, p. 4.

40 David Lyon, Hazard Warning, *Third Way* (London).

41 See particularly Jean Baudrillard's *America*, (Verso, 1988) and the best introduction to Baudrillard's writings in Mark Poster, *Jean Baudrillard: Selected Writings*, (Polity, 1988).

42 Bertens, 1995, p. 146.

43 I am indebted to David Norfield for drawing attention to this illustration during a masters' tutorial at Westminister College, Cambridge.

Chapter Six

1 Bosch, 1991, pp. 264-267.
2 Lawrence Osborn, 1995, on the other hand, identifies five "myths of modernity" that have affected the Church in the West: the myth of evolution, the myth of progress, the myth of objective neutrality, the myth of scientism, and the myth of human perfectibility and autonomy.
3 In ed. Sampson, *et al.*, 1994, p. 27. Such an observation carries considerably implications for the future of Christian ministry in the new millennium.
4 Walker, 1996, p. 74.
5 John Habgood in Ian Bunting (ed.), *Celebrating the Anglican Way*, (Hodder & Stoughton, 1996), p. 34.
6 Stephen Sykes, in ed. Bunting, 1996, p. 25, writes: "In more modern times the critical study of the Bible has been vigorously defended as 'essential to the maintenance in the Church of a healthy faith' (Lambeth Conference of 1897)".
7 Walker, 1996, p. 55.
8 Walker, 1996, p. 51.
9 Quoted in Walker, 1996, p. 51.
10 See both Lesslie Newbigin's *Truth to Tell*, (Eerdmans/World Council of Churches, 1991), and *Proper Confidence*, (Eerdmans, 1995).
11 Harvey, 1990, p. 13.
12 Immanuel Kant, *What is Enlightenment?*, (Liberal Arts Press, 1959), p. 85.
13 By contrast, the Vicar in the later TV comedy series, *The Vicar of Dibley*, is the only sane figure in a zany cast!
14 Radio New Zealand, 16 June, and 27 November 1996.
15 Lyon, 1994, p. 62.
16 P. Berger, From the Crisis of Religion to the Crisis of Secularity, *The Ethics of Authenticity*, (Harvard University Press, 1991), p. 20.
17 For pluralism further refer to: (1) from the point of view of the tradition of academic religious studies Peter Donovan, The Intolerance of Religious Pluralism, in *Religious Studies*, no. 29, 1993, p. 217f; (2) as a deeper study yet rooted in the contemporary situation of the decline of modernity, John

Kekes, *The Morality of Pluralism*, (Princeton University Press, 1991); and (3) in the challenge presented to the Christian faith in our generation, D.A. Carson, Christian Witness in an Age of Pluralism in *God and Culture*, eds. D.A. Carson and J.D. Woodbridge, (Eerdmans, 1993).
18 Newbigin, 1995, p. 48.
19 Middleton and Walsh, 1995, p. 31-2, quoting Jane Flax.
20 During the late 1980s, a controversial New Zealand retired university professor, minister of religion and theological teacher, Prof. Lloyd Geering, in a radio discussion with another Presbyterian, the Rev. Arthur Gunn, between them agreed that they foresaw in the year 2004 the last Presbyterian minister in New Zealand taking the funeral rites of the last Anglican Vicar!

Chapter Seven

1 Noted in Wells, 1993, p 114. Loren Mead develops this general thesis more in *The Once and Future Church*, (Alban Institute (USA), 1991).
2 Walker, 1996, p. 190. See also John Tiller, *A Strategy for the Church's Ministry*, (Church Information Office Publishing (UK), 1983).
3 Wells, 1993, p. 291-300.
4 Postmodernism: Mutual Society in Crisis, *Building a Relational Society*. Graham Cray also refers to Charles Taylor, *Sources of the Self*, (Cambridge, 1989).
5 Walker, 1996, p. 191.
6 James Emery White in Dockery, *The Challenge of Postmodernism*, (Bridgepoint, 1995), p. 364.
7 Acts 2: 47.
8 In New Zealand during the late 1990s the number of churches running Alpha courses increased from 15 in 1995 to over 300 in 1997. Over this same period more than 20,000 people went through an Alpha programme. (Figures provided by the Rev. Ray Muller, Parish Consultant, Anglican Diocese of Wellington, and New Zealand agent for Alpha training and resources.)
9 Cf. Nehemiah 2: 4-5.
10 "The community is as potent a factor in the life of society as either the individual or the state." Jonathan Sachs, *Faith in the Future*, (Darton, Longman & Todd, 1995) p. 56.
11 P. Berger, *A Rumour of Angels*, (Doubleday,

1969), p. 94.

12   Walker, 1996, p. 197.

13   Walker, 1996, p. 198.

14   Walker, 1996, p. 198.

15   Anglican Board of Ministry (UK), Ministry Paper 1.

16   Walker, 1996, p. 195.

17   See, for example, *Celebrating the Anglican Way*, ed. Ian Bunting, (Hodder & Stoughton, 1996), written about the contribution the Anglican Church has to make to "a changing world as we move into a new millennium."

18   The writings of theologian Colin Gunton are significant here, for example his *The One, the Three and the Many*, (Cambridge University Press, 1993).

19   See for example, Romans 8: 18-25, Ephesians 1: 8-10, and Colossians 1: 15-20.

20   Some fundamentalists would identify the Scriptures themselves as the truth in a literal, verbal form, rather than as the locus, focus and agent of the truth of God – as if God had confined himself in the text "like the genie in Aladdin's lamp."

21   James D. Hunter, in ed. Sampson, *et al.*, 1994, p. 28.

22   Walker, 1996, p. 53-4.

23   See the various writings of Jurgen Moltman, particularly *Theology of Hope*, (S.C.M, 1967). Also see Anthony Thistelton, 1995, The Pluriform Grammar of Hope and the God of promise, who identifies hope or promise as that which distinguishes a Christian understanding of the self from either the over-confident trust in the self offered by modernity or the uncentred, unstable self of postmodernity.

24   Keck, 1993, chapter 3.

25   Walker, 1996, p. 190. Walker writes as a member of the Orthodox Church, not as a representative of independency!

26   S. Hauerwas and W.H. Willimon, *Resident Aliens*, (Abingdon, 1989), p. 37.

27   Walker, 1996, p. 189, also writes about the need for Christians "to recapture a sense of civic responsibility, but by being the Church again, and not by attempting to become model citizens of a secular society."

28   In ed. Bunting, 1996, p. 35, 39.

29   Harvey, 1990, p. 41, writes: "The postmodern theological project is to reaffirm God's truth without abandoning the powers of reason."

30   Walker, 1996, p. 53.

31   Keck, 1993, p. 90.

32   Newbigin in ed. Sampson, *et al.*, 1994, p. 70.

33   Keck, 1993, p. 93f.

34   Walker, 1996, p. 119.

35   Wells, 1993, p. 219-32.

36   G.K. Chesterton once made the comment that humility was becoming misplaced. Humility was no longer attached to self-opinion, where it ought to be, but to truth, where it ought not to be.

ALLISON, C. Fitzsimons. 1994, *The Cruelty of Heresy*, SPCK

BAUMAN, Zygmunt. 1992, *Intimations of Postmodernity*, Routledge ***

BERTENS, Hans. 1995, *The Idea of the Postmodern*, Routledge ***

BLAMIRES, Harry. 1963, *The Christian Mind*, Servant,

_____.1980, *Where Do We Stand?*, SPCK

BLOESCH, Donald. 1984, *Crumbling Foundations*, Academic

BLOOM, Alan. 1988, *The Closing of the American Mind*, Penguin *

BOSCH, David. 1991, *Transforming Mission*, Orbis ***

_____. 1995, *Believing in the Future*, Trinity Press

COLSON, Charles. 1989, *Against The Night*, Servant

CRAWSHAW, J. & KIRKLAND, W. (eds). 1994, *New Zealand Made*, Signpost Communications

DAVIS, Brian N. 1995, *The Way Ahead*, Caxton *

DOCKERY, D.S. 1995, *The Challenge of Postmodernism*, Bridgepoint ***

FEATHERSTONE, M. 1991, *Consumer Culture & Postmodernism*, Sage *

GIDDENS, Anthony. 1990, *The Consequences of Modernity*, Polity ***

GRENZ, Stanley. 1996, *A Primer on Postmodernism*, Eerdmans *****

GUINNESS, O. 1983, *The Gravedigger File*, Hodder & Stoughton ***

HART, Trevor. 1995, *Faith Thinking*, SPCK

HARVEY, David. 1990, *The Condition of Postmodernity*, Blackwell **

HAUERWAS, S. & WILLIMON, W.H. 1989, *Resident Aliens*, Abingdon **

HENRY, Carl. 1988, *Twilight of a Great Civilization*, Crossway

HUNSBERGER, G.R. & VAN GELDER, C. (eds). 1996, *The Church Between Gospel and Culture*, Eerdmans ***

HUNTER III, George. 1992, *How To Reach Secular People*, Abingdon

HUNTINGTON, Samuel P. 1996, *The Clash of Civilizations and the Remaking of World Order*, Simon & Schuster ***

KECK, Leander. 1993, *The Church Confident*, Abingdon **

KEW, R. & WHITE, R.J. 1992, *New Millennium, New Church*, Cowley **

KIRK, J. Andrew. 1992, *Loosing the Chains*, Hodder & Stoughton

LYON, David. 1994, *Postmodernity*, Oxford University Press *****

McALPINE, Thomas. 1991, *Facing The Powers*, MARC **

McGRATH, Alistair. 1993, *The Renewal of Anglicanism*, SPCK ****

MEAD, Loren. 1991, *The Once and Future Church*, Alban Institute ***

Bibliography

MIDDLETON, J. & WALSH, B. 1984, *The Transforming Vision*, IVP *

_____. 1995, *Truth Is Stranger Than It Used To Be*, InterVarsity Press ***

MONTEFIORE, H. 1992, *The Gospel & Contemporary Culture*, Mowbray *

MOORE, Peter. 1989, *Disarming the Secular Gods*, InterVarsity Press

NEWBIGIN, Lesslie. 1978, *The Open Secret*, Eerdmans

_____. 1983, *The Other Side of 1984*, World Council of Churches *

_____. 1986, *Foolishness To The Greeks*, SPCK ***

_____. 1989, *The Gospel in a Pluralist Society*, Eerdmans ***

_____. 1991, *Truth to Tell*, Eerdmans/World Council of Churches ****

_____. 1994, *A Word in Season*, Eerdmans/St Andrews ***

_____. 1995, *Proper Confidence*, Eerdmans ****

NOLL, Mark. 1994, *The Scandal of the Evangelical Mind*, Eerdmans

ODEN, Thomas. 1990, *After Modernity...What?*, Zondervan **

OSBORN, Lawrence. 1995, *Restoring The Vision*, Mowbray ****

PATRICK, Bruce (ed.). 1993, *New Vision New Zealand*, Vision *

_____. 1993, *The Vision New Zealand Congress*, Vision

POLKINGHORNE, John. 1994, *Quarks, Chaos & Christianity*, Triangle *

POSTMAN, Neil. 1987, *Amusing Ourselves to Death*, Methuen **

_____. 1993, *Technopoly: the Surrender of Culture to Technology*, Vintage *

SAMPSON, P., SAMUEL, V., & SUGDEN C. 1994, *Faith and Modernity*, Regnum ****

SINE, Tom. 1991, *Wild Hope*, Word **

SIRE, James. 1990, *Discipleship of the Mind*, InterVarsity Press

SNYDER, Howard. 1995, *EarthCurrents*, Abingdon ****

THISELTON, Anthony C. 1995, *Interpreting God and the Postmodern Self*, T&T Clark ***

WALKER, Andrew. 1987, *Enemy Territory*, Hodder & Stoughton **

_____. 1988, *Different Gospels*, Hodder & Stoughton *

_____. 1996, *Telling the Story*, SPCK ****

WALTER, J.A. 1979, *A Long Way From Home*, Paternoster

WELLS, David. 1993, *No Place For Truth*, Eerdmans ****

_____. 1994, *God in the Wasteland*, Eerdmans/InterVarsity Press ****

WRIGHT, Tom. 1992, *New Tasks for a Renewed Church*, Hodder & Stoughton ***

Star System

*****   Essential reading: goes right to the issue in a readable way.

****   Priority reading: admirably sets the issues in a wider context.

***   Significant reading: cannot overlook in gaining the full picture.

**   Very Helpful: good insights from a specific angle.

*   Helpful: contains very useful material.

Index